## REGULATIONS

**Regulation IV (a) – Tee Ball Division:** Added a sentence stating that if a league elects to operate a Tee Ball baseball program only, it must use the league age determination date that is noted in the regulation. Page 33.

**Regulation IV (a) – Junior League:** Added language making it clear that when a 12-year-old player is found to be ineligible under this regulation, that player and/or his/her team are subject to removal from the International Tournament by action of the Tournament Committee. Page 33.

**Regulation VI:** Changes were made to this Regulation and to the Tournament Pitching Rules (Tournament Rule 4). These changes bring the Regular Season and Tournament pitching rules into alignment. Page 38.

**Regulation XIV (e):** Added language making it clear that alcohol is prohibited at the game site. Page 43.

## PLAYING RULES

**Rule 1.10:** Added language making it clear that any bat that has been altered must be removed from play. Page 52.

**Rule 1.11 (k):** Added language making it clear that casts may not be worn by players and umpires during the game, and that persons wearing casts, including managers and coaches, must remain in the dugout during the game. Page 53.

**Rule 1.13 and Rule 1.14:** The size limits on mitts/gloves have been updated to reflect widely accepted norms. Pages 53-54.

**Rule 2.00 Definition of Pitch:** Added language making it clear that a balk or illegal pitch, whether or not a pitch is actually delivered to a batter, counts as a pitch in determining the pitch count for that pitcher. Page 60.

**Rule 3.03 – No. 6:** Added language making it clear defensive substitutions must be made while the team is on defense, and offensive substitutions must be made at the time the offensive player has her/his turn at bat or is on base. (Also added to Rule 3.03 for Big League.) Page 62.

**Rule 5.07, Minor League:** Added language providing that the five-run rule may be suspended in the last half inning for either team, by option of the local league. Page 72.

## TOURNAMENT RULES AND GUIDELINES

**Responsibility and Chain of Command:** Added language making it clear that the Tournament Committee may impose penalties it deems appropriate, or may take action to correct a situation, regardless of the source of information. Page T-2.

**Conditions of Tournament Play – Protests – C. Use of an ineligible player:** Added language making it clear that any violation of Regulations may result in a team having an ineligible player. Page T-12.

**Tournament Rule 4:** Changes were made to this Tournament rule, bringing the Tournament pitching rules into alignment with the Regular Season pitching regulation (Regulation VI – PITCHERS). Page T-13.

## SAFETY

**Appendix A:** Added Lightning Safety Guidelines.
**Appendix D:** Added Bat Modifications and Alterations Policy.

**NOTES**

**Various Regulations, Regular Season Rules, and Tournament Rules:** The deadline for submitting forms that deal with Tournament Eligibility – i.e., regular season player roster forms, Regulation II (d) and Regulation IV (h) forms, waiver requests, chartering, fee payments, combined teams and interleague play forms, etc. – is June 8, 2010.

**Adults and Minors in Positions of Authority:** Changes were made to Rule 2.00, Rule 4.1, Rule 9.01, Rule 9.03, Rule 9.04, and the Tournament Rules and Guidelines, making it clear that Minors may serve as coach or umpire under the specific and limited circumstances as noted.

## CONTENTS

---

# Your League Receives 125 Free Background Checks Per Year

Each year, Little League® International provides 125 free background checks that exceed the minimum standard required in Regulation I(c). Information on how to utilize this benefit, as well as how to conduct background checks, can be found on the Little League website at:

http://www.LittleLeague.org/Learn_More/programs/childprotection.htm

## LITTLE LEAGUE FIELD CENTERS

Little League Field Centers are fully staffed year round to provide assistance and direction to Little League volunteers. All general questions, written suggestions for improving this rulebook, tournament inquiries, rule interpretation requests and supply orders should be directed to the appropriate field center in your region as indicated.

## U.S. REGIONS

**Central Region Hdqts.**
9802 E. Little League Drive
Indianapolis, IN 46235
PHONE: 317-897-6127
FAX: 317-897-6158
E-MAIL:
centralregion@LittleLeague.org

**Eastern Region Hdqts.**
PO Box 2926
Bristol, CT 06011
PHONE: 860-585-4730
FAX: 860-585-4734
E-MAIL: eastregion@LittleLeague.org

**Western Region Hdqts.**
6707 Little League Drive
San Bernardino, CA 92407
PHONE: 909-887-6444
FAX: 909-887-6135
E-MAIL:
westregion@LittleLeague.org

**Southeastern Region Hdqts.\***
PO Box 7557
Warner Robins, GA 31095
PHONE: 478-971-7070
FAX: 478-971-7071
E-MAIL:
southeastregion@LittleLeague.org

**Southwestern Region Hdqts.**
PO Box 20127
Waco, TX 76702
PHONE: 254-756-1816
FAX: 254-757-0519
E-MAIL:
southwestregion@LittleLeague.org

**To access Little League on the Internet:**
**www.LittleLeague.org**

5

**Canadian Region Hdqts.**
235 Dale Avenue
Ottawa, ONT
Canada K1G 0H6
PHONE: 613-731-3301
FAX: 613-731-2829
E-MAIL: canada@LittleLeague.org

**Europe, Middle East and Africa Region Hdqts.**
Little League Europe
Al. Malej Ligi 1
Kutno, 99-300, Poland
PHONE: 011-48-24-254-4569
FAX: 011-48-24-254-4571
E-MAIL: europe@LittleLeague.org

**Latin America Region Hdqts.**
PO Box 10237
Caparra Heights, Puerto Rico  00922-0237
PHONE: 787-982-3076
FAX: 787-982-3076 or 787-728-8164
E-MAIL: latinamerica@LittleLeague.org

**Asia-Pacific Region Hdqts.**
Asia-Pacific Regional Director
C/O Hong Kong Little League
Room 1005, Sports House
1 Stadium Path
Causeway Bay
Hong Kong
PHONE:011-852-2504-4007
FAX:  011-852-2504-8629
E-MAIL: bhc368@netvigator.com

# *LittleLeagueCoach.org* ▼

## Great Coaching
## Starts Here

# Free.

Great coaching is no accident.
It starts with a love for the game.
It grows from a strong desire
to give children the tools they
need to succeed on the field.
And when done right, it teaches
lessons that last a lifetime.

That's why Little League International created LittleLeagueCoach.org – to start you on the path to great coaching. Expert advice from renowned players and coaches; video demonstrations; skills development drills and exercises: At LittleLeagueCoach.org, you can get all the tools you need to start your season right or build on what you already have in place.

## And it's Free.

Little League International considers providing these tools so important to our youth and so important to the success of your team that it has decided to offer them without any charge. Unlike some other youth sports organizations' coaching programs, you won't pay a dime to access the exclusive content and resources at LittleLeagueCoach.org.

Little League®
Coach Resource Center

Sort skills by sport

All | Major Baseball | Minor Baseball | Softball

Role of the Little League Coach

Little League Season Planning

Parental Involvement

Rules of the Game

Teaching the Skills

Drills and Activities

Planning A Practice

Safety, Fitness, and Conditioning

Managing on Game Day

**All anyone has to do is create a FREE account at the Little League Coach Resource Center (www.LittleLeagueCoach.org). Contact your league president or district administrator for more information on creating your account, including the authorization code that is unique to your league. Then log on and start making your season special today!**

# Little League® Coaches Registry Provides Even More Resources

When coaches are ready to take their commitment to coaching Little Leaguers to the next level, the Little League® Coaches Registry makes it possible with even more resources and benefits. Little League® knows that managers and coaches are among the most important volunteers in the Little League® program. They have to know the game and they have to love working with kids. Leagues with knowledgeable, caring and concerned coaches have an advantage when it comes to making the games fun and retaining players.

The Coaches Registry will help them improve their coaching skills, make the games of baseball and softball more fun for the players, and improve the overall effectiveness of the league. The registry gives coaches exclusive tools and resources to prepare them for putting the Little League program into action including searchable electronic rulebooks with video interpretations, training materials and "The Coaches Box" monthly electronic newsletter.

To top it all off, members of the Coaches Registry will receive deep discounts on almost every item purchased through the Little League® online store.

*For more information, log on to www.LittleLeague.org*

## About the Little League-Positive Coaching Alliance Partnership

Entering our third year of national partnership, Positive Coaching Alliance (PCA) and Little League International work to provide a positive, character-building environment for all Little Leaguers.

More than 1,500 Little League coaches throughout the U.S. have completed the online Little League Double-Goal Coach® Course, learning to pursue winning while, more-importantly, teaching life lessons through baseball and softball. The course equips coaches to work with "Second-Goal Parents," PCA's term for sports parents who focus on players' life lessons.

Together, Double-Goal Coaches and Second-Goal Parents develop "Triple-Impact Competitors," who strive to improve themselves, their teammates and their sport. In addition to online coaching and parenting courses, PCA provides dozens of local Little Leagues with comprehensive partnerships designed to ensure that all adults involved in the league are committed to teaching life lessons through baseball and softball.

"This special partnership gives our program's volunteers the tools to teach Little Leaguers much more than just the skills of hitting, throwing and catching a ball," says Stephen D. Keener, president and CEO of Little League Baseball and Softball. "Positive Coaching Alliance's Double-Goal Coach method affords Little League International the opportunity to enhance its educational material for our adult volunteers, so they can present the most well-rounded, healthy and positive experience regardless of skill level."

To take the online Little League Double-Goal Course, visit:
http://www.positivecoach.org/LittleLeague.

To learn more about PCA, visit
http://www.positivecoach.org

## GENERAL INFORMATION
## PURPOSE OF LITTLE LEAGUE BASEBALL AND SOFTBALL

Better than any other youth sport activity, baseball and softball have become the thread that has sewn together a patchwork of nations and cultures around the world. Children in diverse nations such as Israel, Jordan, Ukraine, Germany, Japan, Canada, Hong Kong, Poland, Mexico, China, Venezuela, South Africa and the U.S. have discovered baseball and softball — Little League Baseball and Softball — are ways to bring their people a sport that mirrors life itself.

Baseball and softball embody the discipline of teamwork. They challenge players towards perfection of physical skills and bring into play the excitement of tactics and strategy. The very nature of baseball and softball also teach that while every player eventually strikes out, or is on the losing team, there is always another chance for success in the next at-bat or game.

Millions of children on six continents and more than 80 countries can attest that baseball, softball and Little League are synonymous. Little League is a heritage to be carried forward proudly in the future by ever increasing waves of those devoted to teaching children how to play and enjoy these great games.

Little League is a program of service to youth. It is geared to provide an outlet of healthful activity and training under good leadership in the atmosphere of wholesome community participation. The movement is dedicated to helping children become good and decent citizens. It inspires them with a goal and enriches their lives towards the day when they must take their places in the world. It establishes the values of teamwork, sportsmanship and fair play.

### FEDERAL CHARTER

Little League operates under auspices of the highest recognition that may be accorded to any such organization by the government of the United States. By virtue of legislation approved unanimously by both the House of Representatives and the Senate and signed into law by President Lyndon B. Johnson on July 16, 1964, Little League has been granted a Congressional Charter of Federal Incorporation. No other sports organization has been so honored by the Federal government.

### STRUCTURE

Basically, Little League has three structural components, each dependent upon the other and each vital to the success of the program.

The administrative and service core of the movement is Little League Baseball, Incorporated, a non-profit membership organization that maintains the international program, with International Headquarters in Williamsport, Pennsylvania. Part of the Headquarters structure includes various Regional Headquarters in the U.S. and throughout the world.

The next component is the District. All the leagues within a District (a geographical area usually encompassing 10-20 leagues) elect a District Administrator (DA). The DA and his/her staff of Assistant District Administrators serve as liaisons between the various Regional Headquarters and the local Little Leagues. They are usually the most experienced Little League volunteers in the area, and are charged with helping to ensure that all the volunteers in their districts are well trained, and all the leagues are operating within the guidelines set by Little

League. The District Administrator does not have the authority to suspend, limit or revoke any rules, regulations or privileges of charter by a local Little League, but may recommend such action to the Charter Committee in Williamsport.

The final, most important component is the local Little League. The league provides its services in the community. It furnishes physical facilities, volunteer services and resources to provide a program for children. Through effective leadership and strong administrative policy at the top level, together with training extensions and adherence to rule and policy at District and local league level, Little League is able to provide liberal benefits to children who participate.

## ADMINISTRATION

Little League affairs are administered by the International Board of Directors. Policies, operating procedures and controls of the program are carried out by Little League Headquarters staff, under the direction of the President and the Executive Committee.

The local league operates under a charter granted annually by Little League. The league is autonomous in the sense of having freedom to elect its own officers, finance its program and carry on various other related functions, but it must adhere scrupulously to all rules and regulations established by Little League.

The charter privilege extends use of the name "Little League" and its official insignia to the local Little League. It can be suspended or revoked for violation of rules or regulations by action of the Charter Committee.

## CHARTER COMMITTEE/WAIVERS OF
## RULES AND REGULATIONS

The Charter Committee is a group of personnel at Little League International in Williamsport, Pennsylvania, in whom is placed (by the International Board of Directors) the responsibility of reviewing, granting, suspending or revoking the privileges and conditions of the local league's charter. When a local league wishes to request a waiver of a specific rule or regulation, it must submit the request in writing to the District Administrator, who will forward it with his/her recommendation to the Regional Director. The Regional Director will present the request to the Charter Committee for a decision. No other person or group has the authority to approve waivers of ANY rules or regulations.

## PLAYER ELIGIBILITY

The player must qualify under Little League's definition of residence printed in Section 2 of this book, must be of the correct "league age" for the division, and must have parental consent. Little League offers baseball and softball programs for players league age 5 through 18. Local Little Leagues are encouraged to provide all programs, thus giving all the children in the area a chance to play Little League Baseball or Softball. League age is defined in Regulation IV (a).

## DIVISIONS OF PLAY

Most people know Little League through the Major Division for 9 to 12 year olds. But today Little League provides organized youth sports programs for a wide range of ages. Charter fees are extremely reasonable, with rulebooks and organizational materials provided free.

**Tee Ball Baseball and Tee Ball Softball** programs are for players 5-6 years old (with an option for 7 and/or 8 year olds) who want to learn the fundamentals of hitting and fielding. In Tee Ball, players hit a ball off a batting tee. Rules of the game may be varied to accommodate the need for teaching. The primary goals of Tee Ball are to have fun, to instruct children in the fundamentals of baseball and softball and to allow them to experience the value of teamwork.

**Minor League Baseball and Minor League Softball** programs may be operated within each division for younger players with less experience. The Minor League may be players ages 7-12. Divisions may be established within the Minor League for "machine pitch," "adult pitch" or "player pitch." The goal of the Minor League is to prepare children for eventual selection to a Major Division team.

**Little League Baseball and Little League Softball** (also known as the Major Division) are for players 9 to 12 years old. A league may choose to limit its Major Division to 10, 11 and 12 year olds, or 11 and 12 year olds. The 9-10 Year Old Baseball and Softball Divisions were established as tournament programs to give children the opportunity to experience Tournament Play, up to state level. Leagues may also enter Tournament Play for 11-12 year olds in the Little League Baseball and Little League Softball Divisions, each ending in World Series tournaments.

**Junior League Baseball and Junior League Softball** are established as transitional programs for 12-14 year olds. The programs link the Little League and Senior League divisions and offer a full range of tournament play, including World Series tournaments.

**Senior League Baseball and Senior League Softball** are for players 14 to 16 years old (Senior League Softball 13-16). Both divisions offer a full range of tournament play, including a World Series.

**Big League Baseball and Big League Softball** are programs for players 16 to 18 years old (Big League Softball 14-18) who seek top-level amateur play, each with a full range of tournament play including a World Series.

**The Challenger Division** was established for children ages 5-18 with physical and/or mental disabilities. It also incorporates other children in the league as "buddies" for the Challenger players.

## ROLE OF THE PARENT

The parents of millions of Little Leaguers combined with their children, league officials, umpires, managers, coaches, and countless volunteer agencies including sponsors, represent an imposing cross section of our world. Parents must take the initiative to make the local program successful. Little League is not a club in which membership implies baby-sitting benefits and entertainment privileges.

Practically speaking, Little League is an adult, volunteer work project constructed, supervised and assisted by parents who want to extend this benefit to their children. The parent who shirks this responsibility cannot, in turn, expect others to assume the burden.

Little League developed the Parent Orientation Program to help parents and volunteers better understand the rules and ideals of Little League.

## VOLUNTEER ELIGIBILITY

As a condition of service to the league, all managers, coaches, Board of Directors members and any other persons, volunteers or hired workers, who provide regular service to the league and/or have repetitive access to, or contact with players or teams, must annually complete and submit an official "Little League Volunteer Application" to the local league president. Annual background screenings must be completed prior to the applicant assuming his/her duties for the current season. Refusal to annually submit a fully completed "Little League Volunteer Application" must result in the immediate dismissal of the individual from the local league. (See Regulation 1 (b) and 1 (c) 8 and 9.)

## LEADERSHIP PROGRAMS

In the years ahead there will be millions of children playing Little League Baseball and Softball. Leadership training programs help to widen the scope and improve the standards of leadership at all levels.

### Managers and Coaches

It cannot be stated too strongly that qualified adult volunteers must be enlisted as team managers and coaches. It is not enough that candidates for these important roles have previous experience in the game.

Managers and coaches must possess leadership ability and the know-how to work with young children. Training Little Leaguers in the fundamentals of teamwork, good sportsmanship and discipline are attainable goals, and are readily available through publications, videos, seminars and clinics produced for and by Little League.

Little League® provides a variety of resources to train your league's managers and coaches, including The Little League® Coach Resource Center (www.LittleLeagueCoach.org) and the Little Coaches Registry (www.LittleLeague.org/coaches). The Little League Coach Resource Center is a free online resource that provides expert advice on coaching several different age groups of baseball and softball players, as well as drills that will help coaches better prepare their teams for games. The Little League Coaches Registry, available at a nominal cost, gives managers and coaches access to exclusive resources like electronic rulebooks and training videos, as well as The Coaches Box newsletter, which provides monthly tips and features on topics related to coaching baseball and softball.

Little League also offers guidance on how your league can effectively screen and qualify managers and coaches through the Little League Child Protection Program. Each local league should have a screening process, including background checks and a volunteer application for those who have contact with children. A sample application is included in the publication, "A Year in the Life of Hometown Little League."

### Umpires

Often an overlooked aspect of the Little League program, umpiring is one of the most important. The volunteer umpire is as much a part of Little League as the volunteer manager, coach or concession stand worker.

There is no sound reason for paying umpires, or any other person whose services should be provided on a volunteer basis. Many districts and leagues have found successful ways to operate volunteer umpiring programs, helping to defray the costs that might normally be passed on to the parents.

Little League also offers many training materials, clinics and seminars on umpire education, as well as the Little League Umpire Registry. The registry allows volunteer umpires to receive regular mailings from Headquarters on rule interpretations, updates, etc.

For more information on how to obtain these materials, how to sign up for the Umpire Registry, or on the clinics and seminars nearest you, contact your Regional Headquarters listed on page 4 or 5 of this book or visit www.LittleLeague.org.

## League Officers

Little League offers clinics, seminars and materials to train league officers in all duties. The booklet "A Year in the Life of Hometown Little League" follows a fictional league through a year of operation, showing the right way to solve the most common problems that arise. For information on ordering the booklet, or on attending a seminar, contact your nearest Regional Center, listed on page 4 or 5 of this book.

## INITIATIVES

Little League is more than just bats and balls. It is also a part of life for millions of people every year, so it is important to educate children and adults in other aspects of life as well. Information on the following special projects and initiatives is available from your Regional Headquarters, listed on page 4 or 5 of this book.

**ASAP (A Safety Awareness Program)** — Designed to share the best safety ideas from around the world.

**Little League Urban Initiative** — An initiative to bring baseball to inner-city youths.

**Little League Child Protection Program** — A program to educate local Little League officials, parents and children on ways to stay safe, and how to help ensure people with the proper motives are involved at the local level.

**The Challenger Division** — A division of play for mentally and physically impaired children ages 5-18.

**The Parent Orientation Program** — A program to help parents and volunteers better understand the rules and ideals of Little League, with the goal being to curb unsportsmanlike behavior. Included in this program are a CD-ROM, a video, and a cassette tape.

## RESIDENCE ELIGIBILITY REQUIREMENTS

Each local Little League determines the actual geographic boundaries of the area from within which it shall select players. These boundaries must be described in detail and shown on a map and dated when making application for a Little League charter. Players will be eligible to play with that league only if they reside within the boundaries provided to and approved by Little League Baseball, Incorporated.

A player will be deemed to reside within the league boundaries if:

A. His/her parents are living together and are residing within such league boundaries, OR;

B. Either of the player's parents (or his/her court-appointed legal guardian) reside within such boundaries. It is unacceptable if a parent moves into a league's boundaries for the purpose of qualifying for tournament play.

"Residence," "reside" and "residing" refers to a place of bona fide continuous habitation. A place of residence once established shall not be considered changed unless the parents, parent or guardian makes a bona fide change of residence.

Residence shall be established and supported by documents from THREE OR MORE of the following categories to determine residency of such parent(s) or guardian:

1. Driver's License
2. Voter's Registration
3. School records
4. Welfare/child care records
5. Federal records
6. State records
7. Local (municipal) records
8. Support payment records
9. Homeowner or tenant records
10. Utility bills (i.e., gas, electric, water/sewer, phone, mobile phone, heating, waste disposal)
11. Financial (loan, credit, investments, etc.) records
12. Insurance documents
13. Medical records
14. Military records
15. Internet, cable or satellite records
16. Vehicle records
17. Employment records

Note: Example – Three utility bills (three items from No. 10 above) constitute only ONE document.

It is recommended that the league require some proof of residence within the league's boundaries at the time the player registers. Players and their parents/guardians are advised that a false statement of residence may lead to ineligibility to play Little League Baseball or Softball. Under NO circumstances does ANY person have the authority to grant a waiver that allows a child to play in a local Little League program IN ANY DIVISION, when that child does not qualify under these residency requirements.

If the claim for residency is challenged, three of the above materials must be submitted to Little League Baseball, Incorporated, with an affidavit of residency from the parent(s) or guardian, which shall decide the issue, and that decision will final and binding. Residency documents must illustrate that the residence (as defined above) was inside the league's boundaries for at least one-half of the regular season (as of June 15 of the year in question).

In the case of a Regulation II(d) Waiver Form, or a Regulation IV(h) Waiver Form, the proof of residence for the FORMER residence of the parent(s) that was within the current league's boundaries must be obtained. This proof of residence for the former residence must be supported by the same documentation as noted above.

**Tournament Requirement for Non-Citizens**: *A participant who is not a citizen of the country in which he/she wishes to play, but meets residency requirements as defined by Little League, may participate in that country if:*

1.  his/her visa allows that participant to remain in that country for a period of at least one year, or;
2.  the prevailing laws allow that participant to remain in that country for at least one year, or;
3.  the participant has an established bona fide residence in that country for at least two years prior to the start of the regular season.

Exceptions can only be made by action of the Charter Committee in Williamsport. Any request for a waiver pertaining to the eligibility of a player must be submitted in writing, by the president of the local Little League through the district administrator, to their respective Regional Director not later than the date prescribed in Regulation IV (j). Requests submitted after that date will not be considered.

## PROOF-OF-AGE REQUIREMENTS
### ACCEPTABLE FORMS OF PROOF OF BIRTH DATE

1.  Original proof of age document, if issued by federal, state or provincial registrars of vital statistics in the country in which the Little Leaguer is participating.
2.  If country of participation differs from the country of proof of age document, original proof-of-age document issued by federal, state or provincial registrars of vital statistics, or local offices thereof, are acceptable proof of age, provided the document was filed, recorded, registered or issued within one (1) year of the birth of the child.
3.  An original document issued by federal, state or provincial registrars of vital statistics, or local offices thereof, listing the date of birth, with reference to the location and issue date of the original birth certificate, is acceptable. (The original birth certificate referenced must have been filed, recorded, registered or issued within one (1) year of the birth of the child.) Also issued by these agencies are photocopies of the certificate of live birth with the certification also photocopied, including the signature, and include the seal impressed thereon. Such documents are acceptable without "live" signatures, provided the original filed, recorded, registered or issued date of the birth certificate was within one (1) year of the date of birth.
4.  For children born abroad of a parent or parents who are U.S. citizens, any official government document issued by a U. S. federal agency or service, is acceptable. For military dependents, Department of Defense identification cards and military hospital certificates are acceptable. These must be originals, not copies, and must refer to a filing, recording, registration, or issue date that is within one (1) year of the birth of the child.
5.  A "Statement in Lieu of Acceptable Proof of Birth" issued by a District Administrator is acceptable.

**NOT ACCEPTABLE AS SOLE PROOF OF BIRTH:** Baptismal Certificate; Certificate of Blessing; Certificate of Dedication; Certificate of Circumcision, etc.; Hospital

Certificate; photocopied records; passports.

**Note:** Little League International has authorized the Regional Directors for Latin America, Europe (including Middle East and Africa), and Asia/Pacific, to adopt a policy that excludes No. 1 above. Local Little Leagues and districts in those regions will be informed of the regional policy.

## HOW TO OBTAIN ACCEPTABLE DOCUMENTS
## PROVING DATE OF BIRTH

Certified copy-of-birth records may be obtained from the Registrar of Vital Statistics of each state, province or local office where the child was born. For U.S.-born persons, addresses of these offices or bureaus, fees required, and other pertinent information are supplied by the United States Department of Health and Human Services (National Center for Health Statistics). A database listing the method for obtaining birth records from any U.S. state or territory is available at the following Internet address:

**http://www.cdc.gov/nchs/howto/w2w/w2welcom.htm**

Individual states may also have on-line instructions on how to obtain "rush" birth records. To find out a state's latest policies regarding birth records, go to the Internet site listed below and type "birth records" into the search field, designate the appropriate state, then click on "SUBMIT."

**http://www.firstgov.gov/**

Persons in the U.S. who need a copy of a non-U.S. birth record should contact the Embassy or the nearest Consulate of the country in which the birth occurred. Addresses and telephone numbers for these offices are listed in the U.S. Department of State Publication 7846, "Foreign Consular Offices in the United States," which is available in many local libraries. Copies of this publication may also be purchased from the U.S. Government Printing Office, Washington, DC 20402. Such proof-of-birth records must meet the criteria for acceptable proof listed above.

## HOW TO OBTAIN A
## "STATEMENT IN LIEU OF ACCEPTABLE PROOF OF BIRTH"

When an "Acceptable Proof of Birth" as described previously is not available, then the appropriate number of items in *EACH* of these *FOUR* groups are required so that the participant may obtain a "Statement in Lieu of Acceptable Proof of Birth," which is required for such a participant to be eligible for regular season or tournament play:

**Group 1** – Any one (1) of the following, provided the date of birth is listed: a naturalization document issued by the United States Department of Justice; photocopy of birth certificate; original birth certificate or government record of birth if not containing a filing, recording, registration, or issue date within one (1) year of the date of birth; passport; *PLUS...*

**Group 2** – Any two (2) of the following, provided the date of birth is listed: Baptismal Certificate; Certificate of Blessing; Certificate of Dedication; Certificate of Circumcision; or any other religious-related certificate; Hospital Certificate;

School Record (must be dated, and date of issue must be at least two years prior to current season); Social Security document; Welfare Department document; adoption record. Any item in this group must
be an original document, not a copy; *PLUS...*

**Group 3 –** Any two (2) of the following: A written, signed and notarized statement from...

... the doctor who delivered the child;

... a hospital administrator where the child was delivered;

... the principal or headmaster of the school the child attends;

... a Social Worker with personal knowledge of the child's date of birth;

... a Priest, Rabbi, Minister, Mullah, or other titled religious figure with personal knowledge of the child's date of birth;

... the child's pediatrician or family doctor.

NOTE: In each statement in Group 3, the writer must describe his/her responsibilities or his/ her relationship to the child, and must attest to his/her personal knowledge that the child was born on the date claimed; *PLUS...*

**Group 4 –** A written, signed and notarized statement from one or both parents, or the legal guardian (as appointed by a court of jurisdiction), attesting to the date of birth claimed.

The league president will forward the above documentation to the District Administrator (or, if the team is traveling, the Tournament Director). If in the opinion of the District Administrator, such evidence is satisfactory, a "Statement In Lieu of Acceptable Proof of Birth" will be issued. This statement will be considered to be acceptable proof of age from that point forward, throughout the child's Little League experience, provided all the information submitted is accurate. (Note: If the District Administrator is unable to review the documents, they may be submitted to the appropriate Regional Headquarters.)

**NOTE:** Situations where players use the name of an adopting family or the name of the family with whom they live, but whose births are recorded under the surname of the natural father or mother, will be handled as follows: The president of the league will obtain from the parents or guardian a document that qualifies under Proof-of-Age Requirements, as well as a copy of the adoption papers (if the player has been legally adopted. If the player was not adopted, a notarized statement from the mother and/or father or legal guardian (as appointed by a court of jurisdiction), saying that the player living under one or the other of their surnames is the same player for whom the birth certificate was issued) is also required.

These documents will be submitted to the District Administrator. If the documents are found to be acceptable, a "Statement in Lieu of Acceptable Proof of Birth" will be issued and all original documents returned. The information submitted will be kept confidential.

## FREQUENTLY ASKED QUESTIONS

Here are some answers to the most common questions we receive at Little League International each year.

Q: Can a local Little League program set up an Internet web site in which any of the trademarks of Little League are used?

A: Yes, but only if that site is hosted on "eteamz.com" (a facility approved by Little League Baseball, Incorporated); otherwise by receiving annual written permission from Little League International.

Q: If a manager, coach or umpire is returning from previous years, do they automatically get the same position in the next year?

A: Volunteers in the local Little League program DO NOT HAVE TENURE, regardless of the years of service. In order to serve, a manager, coach or umpire must be appointed by the league president and approved by the local league board of directors annually. Prior service does NOT guarantee re-appointment.

Q: Can a local Little League waive its rights to a player who lives within its boundaries, allowing that player to participate in another Little League program?

A: A local Little League does not have the authority to waive such rights. ONLY THE CHARTER COMMITTEE IN WILLIAMSPORT HAS THIS AUTHORITY. (See "CHARTER COMMITTEE/WAIVERS OF RULES AND REGULATIONS" in the previous section). If the Charter Committee votes to grant a waiver, the District Administrator will be informed in writing. Waivers, if granted, are for the current season only.

Q: Can a child who does not have residence within a league's boundaries play in that league for the regular season only, provided he/she is not eligible for Tournament Play (all stars)?

A: No. However, the local league may request a waiver, listing all circumstances that warrant such a waiver. Only the Charter Committee in Williamsport can make the final decision. (See "CHARTER COMMITTEE/ WAIVERS OF RULES AND REGULATIONS" in the previous section). If the Charter Committee votes to grant a waiver, the District Administrator will be informed in writing. Waivers, if granted, are for the current season only.

Q: If a parent signs a notarized statement granting temporary custody of a child to a friend or other family member, can that friend or family member's residence be used for registering a child to play in Little League?

A: The ONLY acceptable documentation regarding a change of custody is COURT-ORDERED CUSTODY, a decree issued by a judge who has jurisdiction in the matter.

Q: Does the District Administrator have the authority to grant a waiver of a rule or regulation? Example: Could the District Administrator give permission for a local league to register players whose residence is outside the league's boundaries? Could a District Administrator waive ANY rule or regulation?

A: NO. ANY waiver of a rule or regulation can only be made by the Charter Committee in Williamsport. No other person or group has this authority. If the Charter Committee votes to grant a waiver, the District Administrator will be informed in writing. Waivers, if granted, are for the current season only.

Q: What is the required method for selecting Tournament (all star) teams?

A: There is no required method. The local league board of directors decides annually on the selection method. However, a suggested method is included in the Tournament Rules and Guidelines section of this book.

Q: How much does it cost to belong to Little League?

A: The Charter Fee paid once per year to Little League Baseball, Incorporated, by the local Little League, is $16 per team. Two rulebooks for each team chartered are provided free, although the local league president or designated officer may order additional rulebooks at $2 each. Each league must also provide adequate accident insurance coverage. If the league purchases the insurance through Little League, the cost is between $18 and $48 per team, per season, depending upon the location and division of play. Detailed information on the accident insurance offered through Little League is available at your Regional Headquarters.

Q: What is the difference between Regular Season and Tournament Play (all stars)?

A: During the Regular Season, every eligible child in the league's boundaries is given the opportunity to try out and participate on a team. Generally, the Regular Season begins in the spring and can last until September, but the start/end dates for the Regular Season vary. In Tournament Play, a league holding charters in the proper divisions may enter teams In up to five baseball and five softball divisions in the International Tournament. Tournament Play begins around July 1 and ends in late August with World Series tournaments in eight divisions of baseball and softball. Many of the rules and regulations are the same for Regular Season and Tournament Play. However, there are some exceptions, detailed in the Tournament Rules and Guidelines section of this book. Little League also offers a "Second Season" program, sometimes called "Fall Ball" or "Winter League," with details available at your Regional Center, listed on page 4 or 5 of this book.

Q: Can our League or District (or any other level) allow a television station or Internet web site to broadcast or web-cast regular season games, Special Games, or International Tournament games?

A: No. The only authority that can permit this is Little League International. For more information, click on the "Media" section of the Little League web site, www.LittleLeague.org. Information on radio broadcasting can also be found there.

## OFFICIAL REGULATIONS
## LITTLE LEAGUE BASEBALL (MAJORS) DIVISION, MINOR LEAGUE BASEBALL, TEE BALL BASEBALL, JUNIOR LEAGUE BASEBALL, SENIOR LEAGUE BASEBALL, AND BIG LEAGUE BASEBALL

These regulations govern the conduct and operation of chartered Little Leagues.

### I - THE LEAGUE

(a)  The league is the only unit of organization.

1.  The Little League (Majors) Division is to accommodate participants league ages 9-12.

2.  The Minor League Division is an extension of the local Little League to accommodate participants league ages 7 - 12.

3.  The Tee Ball Division is an extension of the local Little League to accommodate participants league ages 5 - 8 and may utilize the batting tee or the pitched ball (by a coach). The league may opt to deliver a designated number of pitches to all batters and then utilize the tee if necessary.

**NOTE 1**: 7 - 8 year-olds may play in Minor League or Tee Ball depending on the local structure and ability of the players.

**NOTE 2**: Players shall not participate in more than one division.

**NOTE 3**: Participants league age 6 are permitted to advance to Minor League Coach Pitch or machine pitch after participation in Tee Ball for one year.

**(b) The league shall be governed by a Board of Directors elected from and by the membership, consisting of volunteer personnel. As a condition of service to the league, all managers, coaches, Board of Directors members and any other persons, volunteers or hired workers, who provide regular service to the league and/or have repetitive access to, or contact with players or teams, must complete and submit an official "Little League Volunteer Application" to the local league president. Annual background screenings must be completed prior to the applicant assuming his/her duties for the current season. Refusal to annually submit a fully completed "Little League Volunteer Application" must result in the immediate dismissal of the individual from the local league. (See also Reg. I (c) 8 and 9.)**

Officers shall be elected by the Board (i.e. president, one or more vice presidents, secretary, treasurer, safety officer, coaching coordinator, and player agent or agents). A president may manage, coach or umpire provided he/she does not serve on the Protest Committee nor serve as tournament team manager or coach. The president will not serve in the capacity of District Administrator. Player agents shall not manage, coach or umpire in their respective divisions. Vice Presidents may manage, coach or umpire provided they do not serve on the Protest Committee.

The President, with approval of Board of Directors, shall appoint managers, coaches and umpires annually. Manager/coach representation on the Board shall not exceed a minority. **NOTE**: All members of the local league Board of Directors, as well as managers and coaches, whose activities in another youth baseball/softball program are deemed detrimental to the operation of the local league, can be removed by a majority vote of the Board of Directors. **Additionally, the local league's Board of Directors has the right to NOT appoint that individual as tournament team manager/coach.**

(c) Each league shall:

1. prepare, adopt and submit to Little League Headquarters, a constitution consistent with all rules, regulations and policies of Little League Baseball, Incorporated.
2. be considered as a separate and not as a division of the same league.
3. apply for and, if approved, be issued a separate charter certificate.
4. have separate boundaries as provided for in Regulation II.
5. adopt and play a separate schedule of games as provided for in Regulation VII. Interleague play and practice with another league(s) may be permitted during the regular season with the **approval of the district administrator. The district administrator must verify that all leagues involved in the interleague combination are properly chartered and insured. Interleague play during the regular season between leagues from two districts must be approved by the regional office. Leagues involved in interleague play will field separate tournament teams. Players shall not be transferred from one league to another. Requests to combine for tournament play must be submitted through the district to the regional offices for approval per guidelines established by Little League. Districts will be required to submit interleague play forms with all insurance claims that result from interleague play.**
6. provide all players with conventional uniforms. Minor League and Tee Ball: T-shirts and caps are recommended, but hand-me-down type uniforms may be worn if so approved by the local Board. (The Official Little League Shoulder Patch must be affixed to the upper left sleeve of the uniform blouse in all divisions of play.).
7. obtain Accident and General Liability insurance.
   A. Accident Insurance coverage is mandatory for all players on all rosters as well as managers, coaches and umpires. The policy must have a minimum coverage of $100,000 per person per accident.
   B. General Liability insurance is mandatory for the league including its volunteers. The policy must have a minimum coverage of $1,000,000 single limit bodily injury and property damage. **The policy must include coverage for claims involving each of the following: 1. athletic participants, and, 2. sexual abuse and molestation.**

   If insurance is purchased locally, a copy of the policy naming "Little League Baseball Incorporated" as an additional Insured must be submitted to Little League International Headquarters with your "Charter Application and Insurance Enrollment" form.

8. **Require that all of the following personnel have annually submitted a fully completed official "Little League Volunteer Application" to the local league president, prior to the applicant assuming his/her duties for the current season: Managers, Coaches, Board of Directors members and any other persons, volunteers or hired workers, who provide regular service to the league and/or have repetitive access to, or contact with, players or teams. The "Little League Volunteer**

Application" must be maintained by the president of the local league board of directors for all personnel named above, for a minimum of the duration of the applicant's service to the league for that year. Failure to comply with this regulation may result in the suspension or revocation of tournament privileges and/or the local league's charter by action of the Charter or Tournament Committee in Williamsport.

9.	Conduct an annual background check on all personnel that are required to complete a "Little League Volunteer Application" prior to the applicant assuming his/her duties for the current season. No local league shall permit any person to participate in any manner, whose background check reveals a conviction or guilty plea for any crime involving or against a minor. A local league may prohibit any individual from participating as a volunteer or hired worker, if the league deems the individual unfit to work with minors.

A local league must conduct a nationwide search that contains the applicable government sex offender registry data.

NOTE 1: Each year, Little League International provides 125 free background checks that exceed the minimum standard required in this regulation. Information on how to utilize this benefit, as well as how to conduct background checks, can be found on the Little League website at:
http://www.LittleLeague.org/Learn_More/programs/childprotection.htm

NOTE 2: The United States Department of Justice National Sex Offender Public Registry is free and available at www.nsopr.gov.

If no sex offender registries exist in a province or country outside the United States the local league must conduct the more extensive of a country, province or city- wide criminal background check through the appropriate governmental agency unless prohibited by law.

Failure to comply with this regulation may result in the suspension or revocation of tournament privileges and/or the local league's charter by action of the Charter or Tournament Committee in Williamsport. If a local league becomes aware of information, by any means whatsoever, that an individual, including, but not limited to, volunteers, players and hired workers, has been convicted of or pled guilty to any crime involving or against a minor, the local league must contact the applicable government agency to confirm the accuracy of the information. Upon confirmation of a conviction for, or guilty plea to, a crime against or involving a minor, the local league shall not permit the individual to participate in any manner.

NOTE: Information regarding background checks is available at www.LittleLeague.org.

(d)	The Little League (Majors) Division may be composed of not more than ten (10) teams, if more than 10 teams are requested, application for a divisional format must be made to the Charter Committee through the District Administrator. If approved, each division must field a separate tournament team.

(e) Not more than one league will be permitted to operate under the same management without expressed recommendation of the District Administrator to Little League Headquarters and subject to final approval by the Charter Committee.

(f) Mergers where there is sufficient enrollment to maintain separate charters shall require the recommendation of the District Administrator to Little League International and be subject to final approval by the Charter Committee.

(g) A local Little League is not permitted to sponsor, administer, underwrite, or otherwise support, any team or teams, any individual or group, for the purpose of participating in a non-Little League Baseball program or event. Violation may result in revocation of charter and/or suspension of tournament privileges. While Little League does not recommend or endorse participation in more than one baseball program, this does not prohibit an individual who plays in a chartered Little League, or a group of such individuals, from participation in a non-Little League program, subject to the provisions of Regulation IV (a) Note 2, and the provisions of the Tournament Rules and Guidelines regarding participation in other programs.

## I – THE LEAGUE: JUNIOR/SENIOR/BIG LEAGUE

(a) Junior League is an extension of the local Little League to accommodate youngsters league ages 13 and 14 **with an exception for 12-year-old players as noted in Regulation IV (a)**; Senior League is an extension of the local Little League to accommodate youngsters league ages 14, 15 and 16; Big League is an extension of the local Little League to accommodate youngsters league ages 16, 17 and 18. **NOTE 1**: This allows the Local League Board of Directors to place some or all 14 year olds in the Junior League Division OR Senior League Division. It also allows the Local League board to place some or all 16 year olds in the Senior League Division OR the Big League Division. **NOTE 2**: Junior/Senior/Big League players may participate in other baseball programs during the regular season and tournament subject to the provisions of Regulation IV.

**Big League**:

Teams from one or more leagues in a district which are currently chartered may join to form a Big League. Any district which can field four (4) teams, must have its own league. Where one district cannot field four (4) teams, leagues in adjoining districts may combine to form a Big League not to exceed ten (10) teams, with approval of the Charter Committee.

**EXCEPTION**: The Big League may be a district-operated program, supervised by the District Administrator. Such a district-wide program may draw participants from within the boundaries of each chartered league in the district. However, each Local League wishing to do so may retain its own team/league structure. Note: District Administrators, even if they operate a district-wide Big League program, are not permitted to vote in the election for District Administrator.

(b) The Junior League and Senior League Divisions shall be governed by the Board of Directors of the local Little League. The Board of Directors of the local Little League shall elect a Player Agent and Vice-President for each division and shall approve the appointment of its managers and coaches annually.

The President may manage, coach or umpire provided he/she does not serve on the Protest Commitee nor serve as tournament team manager or coach. The Player Agent shall not manage, coach or umpire in his/her respective division. Vice President may manage, coach or umpire provided they do not serve on the Protest Committee.

**Big League:**

A local Little League organizing a Big League program of four (4) or more teams shall be governed by the Board of Directors of that league. Where teams of more than one local Little League in a district form a Big League, such league shall be governed by a Board of Directors of representatives of participating leagues. (Local Little League president and player agent may not manage, coach or umpire. Vice President may manage, coach, or umpire provided they do not serve on the Protest Committee.) In the latter event, the District Administrator shall serve as Board Chairman and appoint an assistant to administer the league.

**As a condition of service to the league, all managers, coaches, Board of Directors members and any other persons, volunteers or hired workers, who provide regular service to the league and/or have repetitive access to, or contact with players or teams, must complete and submit an official "Little League Volunteer Application" to the local league president. Annual background screenings must be completed prior to the applicant assuming his/her duties for the current season, Refusal to annually submit a fully completed "Little League Volunteer Application" must result in the immediate dismissal of the individual from the local league.**

(c)  Each division shall operate under the constitution of the local Little League, which Is the only unit of organization. (Big League exception noted above.)

**Big League:**

Each participating local Little League and/or District will:

1. select managers and coaches for its teams;
2. select its players from within the boundaries of the local Little League, or from within the boundaries of chartered leagues participating in the District-wide Big League program;
3. obtain Accident and General Liability insurance.

    Accident Insurance coverage is mandatory for all players on all rosters as well as managers, coaches and umpires. The policy must have a minimum coverage of $100,000 per person per accident.

    General Liability insurance is mandatory for the league including its volunteers. The policy must have a minimum coverage of $1,000,000 single limit bodily injury and property damage. The policy must include coverage for claims arising out of athletic participants.

    If insurance is purchased locally, a copy of the policy must be submitted to Little League Baseball International Headquarters with your "Charter Application and Insurance Enrollment" form.
4. supply uniforms, bats and equipment for its team(s) and contribute proportional costs of baseballs, supplies and operation of program.

5. Require that all of the following personnel have annually submitted a fully completed official "Little League Volunteer Application" to the local league president, prior to the applicant assuming his/her duties: Managers, Coaches, Board of Directors members and any other persons, volunteers or hired workers, who provide regular service to the league and/or have repetitive access to, or contact with, players or teams. The "Little League Volunteer Application" must be maintained by the president of the local league board of directors for all personnel named above, for a minimum of the duration of the applicant's service to the league for that year. Failure to comply with this regulation may result in the suspension or revocation of tournament privileges and/or the local league's charter by action of the Charter or Tournament Committee in Williamsport.

6. Conduct an annual background check on all personnel that are required to complete a "Little League Volunteer Application" prior to the applicant assuming his/her duties for the current season. No local league shall permit any person to participate in any manner, whose background check reveals a conviction or guilty plea for any crime involving or against a minor. A local league may prohibit any individual from participating as a volunteer or hired worker, if the league deems the individual unfit to work with minors.

A local league must conduct a nationwide search that contains the applicable government sex offender registry data.

NOTE 1: Each year, Little League International provides 125 free background checks that exceed the minimum standard required in this regulation. Information on how to utilize this benefit, as well as how to conduct background checks, can be found on the Little League website at:
http://www.LittleLeague.org/common/childprotect/states.asp

NOTE 2: The United States Department of Justice National Sex Offender Public Registry is free and available at www.nsopr.gov.

If no sex offender registries exist in a province or country outside the United States the local league must conduct the more extensive of a country, province or city- wide criminal background check through the appropriate governmental agency unless prohibited by law.

Failure to comply with this regulation may result in the suspension or revocation of tournament privileges and/or the local league's charter by action of the Charter or Tournament Committee in Williamsport.

If a local league becomes aware of information, by any means whatsoever, that an individual, including, but not limited to, volunteers, players and hired workers, has been convicted of or pled guilty to any crime involving or against a minor, the local league must contact the applicable government agency to confirm the accuracy of the information. Upon confirmation of a conviction for, or guilty plea to, a crime against or involving a minor, the local league shall not permit the individual to participate in any manner.

**NOTE: Information regarding background checks is available at www.Little-League.org.**

(d) Each division shall be composed of no more than 10 teams.

(e) On or before April 15, the chartered Little League shall apply for and, if approved, be granted permission to operate a Junior League, Senior League and/or Big League program for the year. On or before April 15, the District shall apply for and, if approved, be granted permission to operate a Big League program for the year.

(f) Boundaries for selection of players shall conform to those of the local Little League. Big League exceptions noted in Regulation I (a).

(g) Each division shall adopt and play a separate schedule of games as provided for in Regulation VII. Interlocking schedules, interleague play or practice shall not be permitted, nor shall players be transferred from one league to another except as provided for in Regulation VII.

(h) Not more than one Junior League or Senior League will be permitted to operate under the same local Little League. However, where a lack of enough player personnel exists and with the recommendation of the District Administrator and approval of the Charter Committee, two or more adjacent chartered Little Leagues comprising not more than 40,000 population of the same district may combine to form one Junior League and/or Senior League. Where two or more leagues have combined to form one Junior League and/or Senior League, a tournament team must be selected from each league, unless an exception is approved by the Charter Committee.

(i) Where two or more Junior and/or Senior Leagues combine, each will make application for charter indicating thereon the number of teams each will field and the need for joint operation. Players from more than one league may be pooled for the purpose of organizing Junior League and/or Senior League teams, with Charter Committee approval.

(j) Where two or more Junior Leagues and/or Senior Leagues combine, the operation shall be governed jointly by the Board of Directors of the Local Leagues. They shall each elect a Vice-President and Player Agent to be in charge of the league(s).

(k) The Vice Presidents will administer the joint Junior League and/or Senior League program subject to the agreement of their Board of Directors and will alternate every other year as Senior Vice-President in charge of the program. The off-year Vice-President will serve as assistant to the Vice-President in charge.

(l) Each Junior League/Senior League will select managers and coaches for its teams.

(m) Each Junior League/Senior League will supply a proportionate number of adult personnel including volunteer umpires.

(n) Each Junior League/Senior League will supply uniforms, bats and playing equipment for its teams and contribute proportionate costs for baseballs, supplies and maintenance of playing field(s). When each league has a field, each will maintain its own.

(o) Each Junior League/Senior League will pay its proportionate share for player accident, liability and volunteer insurance.

## II - LEAGUE BOUNDARIES

(a) Each league shall determine actual boundaries of the area from WITHIN which it shall select players. Only those participants whose residence is within the boundaries of the league shall be eligible to participate. Residence, for the purposes of this regulation, is defined in "Residence Eligibility Requirements" in the first section of this book (Pages 14-16). **NOTE: Any player who does not reside WITHIN the league's boundaries must have an approved waiver issued by the Charter Committee at Little League International. All waiver requests to the Charter Committee must be submitted and approved in writing by the league president before the start of the league's regular season or June 9, whichever occurs first. Requests must be submitted to the regional office through the district administrator.** These boundaries MUST be described in detail AND shown on a map when making application for the charter. The local Little League boundaries shall be the boundaries of the Junior/Senior/Big League. Exception noted for Big League district operating in Regulation I.

(b) When there are two (2) or more leagues within a locale, each must have separate boundaries, detailed by a map. No exception to this provision will be made without written approval of Little League Headquarters.

(c) Team boundaries may be permitted where communities making up a league are widely separated, upon application to and approval by Little League Headquarters.

(d) **The Board of Directors of the Local League, with the approval of the player involved, reserves the right to continue as a player, any individual (1) whose residence changes from within the boundary to outside the league's boundary or (2) who lives outside the league's boundaries because of a revision of such boundaries even if the child then resides in the territory of another league. Current Major League, Minor League or Tee Ball players or any sibling whose brother or sister met the criteria under II (d) at one time may be retained. Any player meeting (1) or (2) above may be retained for the remainder of his/her career, including Little League, Senior and Big League competition. NOTE: A player who qualifies under this regulation and elects not to participate for a playing season is not eligible to be retained for the subsequent season.**
*Regulations II (d) - Processing Procedure*
*The league president will process a II(d) form. Once the president completes the form, he/she must compile "residency requirement" verification that each youngster meets the conditions of II(d) as outlined above. The league president will present this verification to the District Administrator for review. Once the district administrator verifies the documentation meets the regulations, the district administrator will sign the II(d) form granting his or her approval. The league and the district will maintain the form and documentation in their files. This verification process is only required once during a participant's career. The league must maintain this form and documentation for this player for the duration of his/her career until the player graduates from the program or breaks service with the league. Tournament team players will be required to carry a copy of this form and documentation with them throughout the tournament. If*

*contested during tournament play, the league will be required to produce the documentation. Additionally, if it is determined at a later date that the player does not meet the conditions of II(d), the player is ineligible for further participation. Situations in which documentation is not available must be referred to the Charter Committee through the regional office for a decision. The decision of the Charter Committee is final and binding.*

(e) The President (or District Administrator, if the Big League is administered as a district operation) shall, within 14 days after the first regularly scheduled game, give written notice to Little League Headquarters stating the names, dates and conditions pertaining to any player retained under Regulation II (d) and/or IV (h). In the event that such a player is not claimed, the President (or District Administrator, if the Big League is administered as a district operation) of the league shall so notify in writing the player or the President (or District Administrator) of the league within whose boundaries the player now resides.

Such written notice of release shall be given in sufficient time for the player to qualify for tryouts and selection in the league within whose boundaries the player now resides.

(f) Boundaries approved by Little League Headquarters for a chartered league shall be protected. No other league will be chartered to accept player candidates from all or any part of the same territory for that calendar year. When necessary the District Administrator shall have the authority to adjust the league boundaries and be subject to review and approval of the Charter Committee.

(g) **Upon approval of the International Board of Directors, each local Little League's boundaries will be "frozen" at its current status. "Frozen" means, each league will continue to operate under its current boundaries. The league shall limit its boundaries to and draw its players from an area approved by the District Administrator and Regional Director. Boundary maps for leagues must be signed and dated by the League President and District Administrator with a copy to be sent to the Regional Office. The approved map on file at the Regional Office is the "official" map, provided it does not encroach on any other chartered Little League's boundary. The Charter Committee reserves the right to grant waivers and adjust boundaries where needed. All requests for mergers and to expand league boundaries by adding additional territory must be provided to the Charter Committee through the District Administrator and Regional Director. The decision of the Charter Committee on these requests is final and binding.**

**NOTE 1: Each league will be required to have a current boundary map, approved by the District Administrator, in the regional office files. This will be required for tournament privileges for the current season.**

**NOTE 2: All leagues currently operating under a divisional format must continue to operate under this method. Exceptions to the divisional format can only be granted by the Charter Committee in Williamsport.**

**Note 3: Any request for newly chartered leagues will be reviewed by the**

**Charter Committee under this regulation before a charter is granted. The decision of the Charter Committee is final and binding.**

## III - THE TEAMS

(a)  The league shall, at least 10 days prior to the first regular game, establish the number of players on each team. No team may have more than 15 players (18 for Big League) nor less than 12. **Minor League** and **Tee Ball: There will be no minimum or maximum established at the Minor League and Tee Ball levels.**

NOTE: If a local league elects to roster less than nine (9) players at the Tee Ball and/or Minor League levels, rules 3.03 Note 2, 4.16 and 4.17 do not apply.

The manager of a team must, at least five days prior to the first regularly scheduled game, register the regular team roster. All teams in a particular division must carry the same number of players on their rosters.

(b)  No more than the number of players established by the league under Regulation III, Section (a) may be in uniform during any game. Batboys and/or batgirls are not permitted.

(c)  **Little League (Majors) Division**: Local League must establish the age structure for the Little League (Majors) Division. At no time shall a team have on its roster more than eight players whose league age is 12. Balance of the team roster shall be comprised of players whose league age is 9, 10 or 11. For Junior/Senior/Big League, It is recommended that the local Little League (or district, if the Big League is administered as a district operation) set a maximum and/or minimum number of participants of a particular league age. (Example: If the league has all 15 and 16 year olds in its Senior League Division, it may have a local rule that states that each team must carry between four and eight players of league age 16.)

**Minor League**: Local League must establish the age structure for the Minor League Division. The Minor League may be sub-divided into Minor League Coach Pitch, Minor League Machine Pitch and/or Minor League Player Pitch divisions, with the method for division determined by the local Little League Board of Directors. A player listed on a Little League (Majors) Division roster shall not be permitted to play with a Minor League team.

**Tee Ball**: Local League must establish the age structure for the Tee Ball Division. Players league age 5 and 6 are eligible only for Tee Ball. Exception: Participants league age 6 are permitted to advance to Minor League Coach Pitch or machine pitch after participation in Tee Ball for one year.

A player listed on a Tee Ball roster shall not be permitted to play with a Minor League team.

(d)  If a team loses any player(s) on the roster during the current season through illness, injury, change of address, or other justifiable reasons (subject to Board approval), another player shall be obtained through the player agent, to replace the one lost. The playing ability of the child shall not be considered a justifiable reason for replacement. Such replacement must be of such league age as to comply with Section (c) of this Regulation, and must be eligible under all sections of Regulation IV. The Local League (or district, if the Big League is administered as a district operation) should specify in its

31

local rules the number of days allowed for a manager to comply with selection of a replacement. When changes are desired, the following procedures must be followed:

1. Manager shall acquaint the Board of Directors of the Local League (or district, if the Big League is administered as a district operation) with the conditions which necessitate the request for a replacement.

2. If the majority of the Board of Directors (or district, if the Big League is administered as a district operation) agrees that the reasons are justifiable, the manager may call up a replacement who is eligible under Regulation III, Section (c) and all sections of Regulation IV.

   **NOTE 1**: A league (or district, if the Big League is administered as a district operation) may adopt a local rule prohibiting replacements from the Minor League program onto a Little League (Majors) Division team during the last two weeks of the regular season schedule.

   **NOTE 2**: When a player misses more than seven (7) continuous days of participation for an illness or injury, a physician or other accredited medical provider must give written permission for a return to full baseball activity.

(e) Managers may request to release players for any justifiable reason (as in (d) above, subject to Board approval) between the conclusion of one season and seven (7) days prior to the tryout session, but not later than the players selection or draft meeting of the subsequent season. In the event that a player is released, the president of the league (or district, if the Big League is administered as a district operation) shall notify the player agent, and the player in writing. Such written notice of release shall be given in sufficient time for the player to qualify for tryouts and selection to another team.

**Minor League and Tee Ball**: If a team manager loses any players on the roster during the current season through illness, injury, change of address, or other justifiable reasons (subject to Board approval), another player could be transferred within that Division, through the player agent, to replace the one lost, or a player may be obtained, through the player agent, from a list of children who registered after teams were formed.

**NOTE 1**: Minor League and Tee Ball players may be reassigned at the discretion of the local League Board of Directors and player agent in order to provide a balanced training program.

**NOTE 2**: Minor League and Tee Ball teams must be dissolved at the end of the current season, with all players being returned to a player pool.

## IV - THE PLAYERS

(a) **Little League (Majors) Division**: Any candidate who will attain the age of 9 years before May 1 and who will not attain the age of 13 before May 1 of the year in question shall be eligible to compete in Little League Baseball (subject to the Local League Board of Directors alignment of this division). This means that a child who will be 13 years old on May 1 or later, is eligible to play that year; a child who will be 13 years old on April 30 or earlier will not be eligible for either Local League play or tournament play at any time during the calendar year in question.

**Minor League Division**: Any candidate who will attain the age of 7 years before May 1 and who will not attain the age of 13 before May 1 of the year in question shall be eligible to compete in the Minor League Division Baseball (subject to the Local League Board of Directors alignment of this division). This means that a child who will be 13 years old on May 1 or later, is eligible to play that year; a child who will be 13 years old on April 30 or earlier will not be eligible for either Local League play or tournament play at any time during the calendar year in question.

**Tee Ball Division**: Any candidate who will attain the age of 5 years before May 1 and who will not attain the age of 9 before May 1 of the year in question shall be eligible to compete in the Tee Ball Division Baseball (subject to the Local League Board of Directors alignment of this division). This means that a child who will be 9 years old on May 1 or later, is eligible to play that year; a child who will be 9 years old on April 30 or earlier will not be eligible for either Local League play or tournament play at any time during the calendar year in question.

**NOTE: If a league elects to operate a Tee ball baseball program only, it must use the league age determination date noted above.**

**Junior League**: Any youngster who will attain the age of 13 years before May 1 and who will not attain the age of 15 years before May 1 of the year in question shall be eligible to compete. This means that a youngster who will be 15 years old on May 1 or later is eligible to play that year; a youngster who will be 15 years old on April 30 or earlier will not be eligible for either Local League or tournament play in the Junior League at any time during the calendar year in question.

*A 12-year-old player who is otherwise eligible under all conditions would be eligible for selection to the Junior League Division tournament team. However, a local Little League's board of directors could decide that players league-age 12 in the league will not try out for the Junior League Division, and will be eligible for only the Little League ("Majors") Division/Minor League Division.*

*If a player is selected to and/or participates in one or more regular season games on a Junior League team, he/she will be ineligible to participate in the Major Division from that point forward in regular season and/or tournament play. During International Tournaments, a player deemed ineligible under this regulation is subject to removal and his/her team is subject to forfeiture by action of the Tournament Committee.*

*Regarding a player who moves up the Junior League Division during the season, to be eligible for selection to the Junior Division Tournament team, the player would have to play in sixty (60) percent of the Regular Season games for which he/she was eligible, as of June 15.*

*Any player who is league age 12 must be permitted to play in the Major Division. The local league cannot force any player who is league age 12 to play in the Junior League Division.*

**Senior League**: Any youngster who will attain the age of 14 years before May 1 and who will not attain the age of 17 years before May 1 of the year in question shall be eligible to compete. This means that a youngster who will be 17 years old on May 1 or later is eligible to play that year; a youngster who will be 17 years old on April 30 or earlier will not be eligible for either

Local League or tournament play in the Senior League at any time during the calendar year in question.

**Big League**: Any youngster with amateur status who will attain the age of 16 years before May 1 and who will not attain the age of 19 years before May 1 of the year in question shall be eligible to compete. This means that a youngster who will be 19 years old on May 1 or later is eligible to play that year; a youngster who will be 19 years old on April 30 or earlier will not be eligible for either Local League or tournament play in the Big League at any time during the calendar year in question.

**NOTE**: Little League (Junior/Senior/Big League) accident insurance covers only those activities approved or sanctioned by Little League Baseball, Incorporated.

A unit Little League (Majors), Minor League, Tee Ball, or Junior/Senior/Big League team shall not participate as a Little League (Majors), Minor League, Tee Ball or Junior/Senior/Big League team in games with other teams of other programs or in tournaments except those authorized by Little League Baseball.

Little League (Majors), Minor League, Tee Ball and Junior/Senior/Big League participants may participate in other programs during the Little League (Majors), Minor League, Tee Ball and Junior/Senior/Big League regular season provided such participation does not disrupt the Little League (Majors), Minor League, Tee Ball and Junior/Senior/Big League season.

**NOTE 1: See Tournament Rules, Page T-4 ("Participation in Other Programs"), regarding participation in non-Little League programs during the International Tournament ("All-Stars").**

**NOTE 2**: Consistent with a manager's ability to conduct the affairs of his or her team, a manager may remove a player from the team, subject to Board of Directors approval (or district approval, if the Big League is administered as a district operation), for the current season if the player repeatedly misses practice or games. If a player is repeatedly missing practices or games, the manager must make the Local League Board of Directors aware of the situation immediately.

(b)     Each candidate must present acceptable proof of age to the league president (or District Administrator, if the Big League is administered as a district operation) at least 48 hours before the player selection plan is put into operation. When and if such formal proof of age is not available, the league president shall gather as much documentary evidence as possible and promptly forward it to the District Administrator. If, in the opinion of the District Administrator, such evidence is satisfactory, a statement to that effect will be sent to the league president, which shall be acceptable in lieu of a birth certificate. Such statement will be held in the local Little League files (or district files, if the Big League is administered as a district operation) as acceptable proof-of-age.

(c)     The president of the Local League (or District Administrator, if the Big League is administered as a district operation) MUST certify and be responsible for the eligibility of each candidate previous to player selection. Note: At the time of registration, a player must designate whether he or she will try out for baseball or softball. No player may be on the roster of more than one team or league in the Little League program.

(d) The "League Age" of each candidate shall be recorded and announced at the player selection to guide the managers in making their selections.

(e) "League Age" is that age attained prior to May 1 in any given season. Thus, a child whose 12th birthday is on April 30 or earlier has a League Age of 12; a child whose 12th birthday is on May 1 or later has a League Age of 11. This principle applies regardless of age.

(f) **Little League (Majors) Division and Junior/Senior/Big League**: Any candidate failing to attend at least 50 percent of the spring tryout sessions, shall forfeit league eligibility unless an excuse is presented which is accepted by a majority of the Board of Directors (or district, if the Big League is administered as a district operation).

**Minor League and Tee Ball**: Any eligible player who qualifies and becomes available after player assignment should be assigned to a team.

**NOTE**: A Local League should accept registrations until the time of player selections. Thereafter, registration may be closed.

(g) Player roster forms supplied by Little League Headquarters must be completed and filed no later than June 8, 2010. Players claimed under Regulation II (d) and/or IV (h) must be declared on appropriate forms available from Little League Headquarters annually. It is highly recommended that rosters be supplied to Headquarters via the Little League Data Center. Look for related information online at www.LittleLeague.org.

(h) If a person had previously resided within the league boundaries for two years or more while serving that league as a dedicated manager, coach or member of the Local League Board of Directors for two or more years, his or her sons and/or daughters are eligible to try out and be selected by teams in that league (1) provided such service to the league from which the person has moved has continued, (2) subject to written agreement from the league within whose boundaries they currently reside and (3) and approved by the District Administrator.

*Regulation IV(h) – Processing Procedure*
*The league president will process a IV(h) form. Once the president completes the form, he/she must compile "residency requirement" verification that each youngster meets the conditions of IV(h) as outlined above. The league president will present this verification to the District Administrator for review. Once the district administrator verifies the documentation meets the regulations, the district administrator will sign the IV(h) form granting his or her approval. The league and the district will maintain the form and documentation in their files. This verification process is only required once during a participant's career. The league must maintain this form and documentation for this player for the duration of his/her career until the player graduates from the program or breaks service with the league. Tournament team players will be required to carry a copy of this form and documentation with them throughout the tournament. If contested during tournament play, the league will be required to produce the documentation. Additionally, if it is determined at a later date that the player does not meet the conditions of IV(h), the player is ineligible for*

*further participation. Situations in which documentation is not available must be referred to the Charter Committee through the regional office for a decision. The decision of the Charter Committee is final and binding.*

(i) Every rostered player present at the start of a game will participate in each game for a minimum of six (6) defensive outs and bat at least one (1) time. Big League: Mandatory play does not apply.

**PENALTY**: The player(s) involved shall start the next scheduled game, play any previous requirement not completed for Section (i) and the requirement for this game before being removed.

The manager shall for the:

A. First Offense - receive a written warning.

B. Second Offense - a suspension for the next scheduled game.

C. Third Offense - a suspension for remainder of the season.

**NOTE 1**: If the violation is determined to have been intentional, a more severe penalty may be assessed by the Board of Directors. However, forfeiture of a game may not be invoked.

**NOTE 2**: There is no exception to this rule unless the game is shortened for any reason, at which time the Local League may elect not to impose a penalty on the manager/coach.

**NOTE 3**: In Minor League, if a half-inning ends because of the imposition of the five-run limit in "Rule 2.00 - Inning," and a player on the defense has played for the entire half-inning, that player will be considered to have participated for three consecutive outs for the purposes of this rule. However, if the player has not played on defense for the entire inning, that player will be credited only as having played for the number of outs that occurred while the player was used defensively.

**Big League:** Mandatory play does not apply.

**Minor League and Tee Ball**: If a league uses 15 to 20 player rosters they may reduce the Mandatory Play Rule to three (3) defensive outs and one (1) at bat per game.

(j) Any request for a waiver pertaining to the eligibility of a player, team, manager, or coach must be submitted in writing, by the president of the local Little League through the district administrator, to their respective Regional Director not later than June 9 of the current year. Requests submitted after that date will not be considered.

## AGE ALIGNMENT FOR JUNIOR LEAGUE, SENIOR LEAGUE AND BIG LEAGUE

At the Little League 22nd International Congress in Ottawa, Ontario, Canada, in 2001, District Administrators voted overwhelmingly to alter the age structure in the Junior League, Senior League and Big League Divisions. The new age structure allows greater flexibility in these divisions and is intended to increase participation.

The objectives are: 1. To allow leagues with enough personnel to have a two-year age structure, while smaller leagues could retain a three-year structure for Senior League and/or Big League, and; 2. To aid in the retention of players in all age groups, particularly 13 and 16 year olds.

Under the new structure, Big League Baseball will remain available to 16, 17 and

18 year olds. However, with the 14 year olds and 16 year olds being the "swing" ages, a league COULD structure its program this way: Junior League 13-14; Senior League 15-16; Big League 16-18.

The table below gives each of the possible combinations allowable under the new regulations. However, if a Local League wishes to allow the Junior Division to include 15 year olds in Regular Season play, it must request permission in writing from the Charter Committee. Under no circumstances will a league be permitted to operate a division that includes 13-16 year olds.

|          | Junior League | Senior League | Big League |
|----------|---------------|---------------|------------|
| League A | 13, 14        | 15, 16        | 17, 18     |
| League B | 13, 14        | 14, 15, 16    | 17, 18     |
| League C | 13, 14        | 14, 15, 16    | 16, 17, 18 |
| League D | 13, 14        | 14, 15        | 16, 17, 18 |
| League E | 13, 14        | 15, 16        | 16, 17, 18 |
| League F | 13            | 14, 15, 16    | 16, 17, 18 |
| League G | 13            | 14, 15, 16    | 17, 18     |
| League H | 13            | 14, 15        | 16, 17, 18 |

**NOTE**: Players league age 12 are eligible for the Junior League division at the option of the local league board of directors. Any player who is league age 12, and who plays in one or more games during the regular season at the Junior League level, is eligible only for selection to the Junior League Division Tournament Team.

The structure for Tournament Play is: 9-10 Year Old Division (9-10); 10-11 Year Old Division (10-11); Little League Division (11-12); Junior League Division (12-13-14); Senior League Division (14-15-16); Big League Division (16-17-18).

## V - SELECTION OF PLAYERS

(a) The selection of players for the various teams within a league shall be in compliance with the Little League Draft Selection System as detailed in the Operating Manual. **NOTE**: All candidates who are league age twelve (12) must be drafted to a Major Division team. Exceptions can only be made with written approval from the *District Administrator*, and only if approved at the local league level by the Board of Directors and the parent of the candidate.

(b) When a league decides to substitute a selection system for the one advocated by Little League Baseball, Incorporated, a complete description of such substituted system MUST BE PRESENTED in writing FOR APPROVAL when applying for a charter.

(c) **Alternate method of operation**

To aid leagues that are having a difficult time getting enough players for their regular season teams the following option is available:

A pool of players from existing regular season teams can be created with players that are willing to participate in extra games during the regular season when teams face a shortage of rostered players for a regular season game. **NOTE**: Players may not be "borrowed" from an opponent. They must be assigned by the Player Agent.

**Guidelines**:

1. The league's Player Agent will create and run the pool. The league's Player Agent will use the pool to assign players to teams that are short of players on a rotating basis.

2. Managers and/or coaches will not have the right to randomly pick and choose players from the pool.

3. Under this option, when a player participates in a game on a team other than his/her own team, such player will not be permitted to pitch in that game.

4. Pool players that are called and show up at the game site must play at least nine consecutive defensive outs and bat once.

(d) Teams are not permitted to enter the Little League program intact, or nearly intact, from non-Little League programs. Under no circumstances will any team or group of players, which did not play on the same team for the previous regular season in the same division of a chartered local Little League, be placed together onto a regular season team in that local Little League. Such players must be processed through the Little League Draft Selection System as noted in this regulation.

## VI - PITCHERS

(a) Any player on a regular season team may pitch. (**NOTE**: There is no limit to the number of pitchers a team may use in a game.)

(b) A pitcher once removed from the mound cannot return as a pitcher. Junior, Senior, and Big League Divisions only: A pitcher remaining in the game, but moving to a different position, can return as a pitcher anytime in the remainder of the game, but only once per game.

(c) The manager must remove the pitcher when said pitcher reaches the limit for his/her age group as noted below, but the pitcher may remain in the game at another position:

| League Age | | |
|---|---|---|
| | 1 7-18 | 105 pitches per day |
| | 13 -16 | 95 pitches per day |
| | 11 -12 | 85 pitches per day |
| | 9-10 | 75 pitches per day |
| | 7-8 | 50 pitches per day |

**Exception**: Exception: If a pitcher reaches the limit imposed in Regulation VI (c) for his/her league age while facing a batter, the pitcher may continue to pitch until any one of the following conditions occurs: 1. That batter reaches base; 2. That batter is put out;

3. The third out is made to complete the half-inning. **Note 1: A pitcher who delivers 41 or more pitches in a game cannot play the position of catcher for the remainder of that day.**

(d) Pitchers league age 14 and under must adhere to the following rest requirements:

• If a player pitches 66 or more pitches in a day, four (4) calendar days of rest must be observed.

• If a player pitches 51 - 65 pitches in a day, three (3) calendar days of rest must be observed.

• If a player pitches 36 - 50 pitches in a day, two (2) calendar days of rest must be observed.

• If a player pitches 21 - 35 pitches in a day, one (1) calendar days of rest must be observed.

• If a player pitches 1-20 pitches in a day, no (0) calendar day of rest is required.

**Pitchers league age 15-18 must adhere to the following rest requirements:**

• If a player pitches 76 or more pitches in a day, four (4) calendar days of rest must be observed.

• If a player pitches 61 - 75 pitches in a day, three (3) calendar days of rest must be observed.

• If a player pitches 46 - 60 pitches in a day, two (2) calendar days of rest must be observed.

• If a player pitches 31 -45 pitches in a day, one (1) calendar days of rest must be observed.

• If a player pitches 1-30 pitches in a day, no (0) calendar day of rest is required.

(e) Each league must designate the scorekeeper or another game official as the official pitch count recorder.

(f) The pitch count recorder must provide the current pitch count for any pitcher when requested by either manager or any umpire. However, the manager is responsible for knowing when his/her pitcher must be removed.

(g) The official pitch count recorder should inform the umpire-in-chief when a pitcher has delivered his/her maximum limit of pitches for the game, as noted in Regulation VI (c). The umpire-in-chief will inform the pitcher's manager that the pitcher must be removed in accordance with Regulation VI (c). However, the failure by the pitch count recorder to notify the umpire-in-chief, and/or the failure of the umpire-in-chief to notify the manager, does not relieve the manager of his/her responsibility to remove a pitcher when that pitcher is no longer eligible.

(h) Violation of any section of this regulation can result in protest of the game in which it occurs. Protest shall be made in accordance with Playing Rule 4.19.

(J) A player who has attained the league age of twelve (12) is not eligible to pitch in the Minor League. (**See Regulation V – Selection of Players**)

(k) A player may not pitch in more than one game in a day. (Exception: In the Big League Division, a player may be used as a pitcher in up to two games in a day.)

**NOTES** :

1. The withdrawal of an ineligible pitcher after that pitcher is announced, or after a warm-up pitch is delivered, but before that player has pitched a ball to a batter, shall not be considered a violation. Little League officials are urged to take precautions to prevent protests. When a protest situation is imminent, the potential offender should be notified immediately.

2. Pitches delivered in games declared "Regulation Tie Games" or "Suspended Games" shall be charged against pitcher's eligibility.

3. In suspended games resumed on another day, the pitchers of record at the time the game was halted may continue to pitch to the extent of their eligibility for that day, provided said pitcher has observed the required days of rest.

**Example 1**: A league age 12 pitcher delivers 70 pitches in a game on Monday when the game is suspended. The game resumes on the following Thursday. The pitcher is not eligible to pitch in the resumption of the game because he/she has not observed the required days of rest.

**Example 2**: A league age 12 pitcher delivers 70 pitches in a game on Monday when the game is suspended. The game resumes on Saturday. The pitcher is eligible to pitch up to 85 more pitches in the resumption of the game because he/she has observed the required days of rest.

**Example 3**: A league age 12 pitcher delivers 70 pitches in a game on Monday when the game is suspended. The game resumes two weeks later. The pitcher is eligible to pitch up to 85 more pitches in the resumption of the game, provided he/she is eligible based on his/her pitching record during the previous four days.

**Note**: The use of this regulation negates the concept of the "calendar week" with regard to pitching eligibility.

## VII - SCHEDULES

(a)  The schedule of games for the regular season shall be prepared by the Board of Directors of the league **(or district, if the Big League is administered as a district operation)** and must provide for not less than twelve (12) games per team per regular season, exclusive of playoff and tournament games.

(b)  The schedule should provide for not less than two (2) games per week per team. **Junior League and Senior League: Interleague play is permitted provided the proper form is submitted to the Regional Director through the District Administrator for approval. Big League: Interleague play is permitted within the district.**

(c)  Where there are two (2) or more leagues in one locality, teams of one league shall not play teams of another league, without approval of the District Administrator, Regional Director and the Charter Committee (see Reg. I (c) 5).

(d)  **Little League (Majors) Division**: A team may play one (1) doubleheader in a calendar week. No team shall play three games in a day. (Exception under condition of Rule 4.12.)
**Minor League and Tee Ball**: No team shall be scheduled to play two games in one day. (See Rule 4.12).
**Junior/Senior/Big League: doubleheaders are permitted.**
If two games involving four teams are played on the same day and on the same field, the first game must be completed before the second game starts. (Exception under condition of Rule 4.12.)
When League size and limited field availablility require leagues to schedule more than one game on the same night and on the same field, the league may be permitted to impose a time limit on the first game. However, the game must meet the requirements of Rule 4.10 or 4.11 to be official.

(e)  The schedule shall be arranged so that at least one-half of the games are scheduled prior to June 15.

(f)  **Little League (Majors), Junior/Senior/Big League**: It is recommended that a split season schedule be arranged with a playoff between the winners of the first and second halves to determine the league champion. **Junior/Senior/ Big League: When approval is granted for two or more leagues - comprising not more than 40,000 population - to form one Junior League or Senior League, as provided for in Regulation I (h), one regular-season schedule will be prepared by a joint committee from the two or more leagues.**

(g) All play must be terminated by the opening date of school for the fall term but no later than September 1st unless participating in the Training and Development Program.

(h) **Little League (Majors) Division**: There shall be no time limit on games. (Exception under Regulation X (c)).

**Minor League and Tee Ball**: A Local League may impose a time limit on games regardless of the number of innings played. It is recommended that no league standings be kept, and no championship games be played.

## VIII - MINOR LEAGUES
(Does not apply to Junior/Senior/Big League.)

(a) The purpose of the Minor League program is to provide training and instruction for those candidates who by reason of age and other factors do not qualify for selection in the regular Little League.

(b) The Minor League program is the responsibility and is an integral part of the chartered Little League. It is not and may not be operated as a separate entity. It must be restricted to the boundaries of the Local League and its players are subject to selection by draft by any Little League (Majors) Team of the Local League. Refusal of a player to comply shall result in forfeiture of further eligibility in the Little League (Majors) Division for the current season.

**Note**: The Local League should establish a policy, approved by the Board of Directors, regarding players who decline to move up to a major league team. Such policy should be distributed at the time of registration and/or tryouts.

(c) No player or team may be deemed to be the property of, or under the jurisdiction or control of, a particular team in the Local League.

(d) A Local League may elect to utilize adult pitch ("Minor League Coach Pitch") or machine pitch ("Minor League Machine Pitch") in Minor League games involving players league ages 7-12. Pitching machines, if used, must be in good working order and must be operated by adult managers, coaches, umpires or any adult approved by the local league.

Note: Participants are permitted to advance to Minor League Coach Pitch or machine pitch after participation in Tee Ball for one year.

## IX - SPECIAL GAMES

(a) Special Games are defined as games that:
1. are non-regular season games, and,
2. are not Little League International Tournament games, and,
3. involve only teams from chartered Little league programs, and,
4. have been approved in writing by the regional office.

(b) Unless expressly authorized under conditions of this Regulation, games played for any purpose other than to establish a league champion (or district champion, if the Big League is administered as a district operation) or as part of the International Tournament are prohibited. Violation may result in revocation of charter and/or suspension of tournament privileges.

(c) With the approval of the Charter Committee of Little League Headquarters, and on recommendation of the Regional Director and District Administrator, chartered leagues may engage in Special Games during and after the regular season but prior to the opening of the school term or September 1st, whichever comes sooner.

(d) Special Games may be played between:
1. Regular season teams or;
2. All-Star teams using either regular season or tournament rules, but not in combination.

(e) Teams participating in Special Games during the regular season shall be regular season teams only. Tournament teams, regular season teams and Minor League teams involving players below league age 11 may use 9-10 Year Old Division tournament rules.

(f) Tournament teams may participate in Special Games only following elimination from the International Tournament.

(g) The league president will be charged with responsibility for conducting special games under all rules, regulations and policies of Little League Baseball.

(h) This rule does not prohibit pre-season practice games between teams in the same division in the same league or the practicing of the league's tournament team against other players in the same division in the same league, provided such practice is done out of uniform.

(i) **Tee Ball**: Special Games are permissible only with regular season teams. However, they are not recommended by Little League Headquarters. "All Stars" are not authorized.

## X - NIGHT GAMES

(a) Little League (Majors) Division, Minor League, Tee Ball, Junior, Senior and Big League games may be played after sundown under artificial lights. This responsibility shall rest with the Local Leagues. In any event, no inning shall start after 10:00 p.m. prevailing time (9:00 p.m. for Tee Ball; **10:30 p.m. for Junior and Senior; 11 p.m. for Big League)**. It will be held that an inning starts the moment that the third out is made, completing the preceding inning.

(b) Artificial lights for Little League games must meet the minimum standards approved by Little League Baseball. (See Operating Manual for standards.)

(c) When league size and limited field availability require leagues to schedule more than one game on the same night and on the same field, the league may be permitted to impose a time limit on the first game. However, the game must meet requirements of Rule 4.10 or 4.11 to be official.

## XI - ADMISSION TO GAMES

No admission shall be charged to any Little League (Majors) Division, Minor League or Tee Ball game. Voluntary contributions are permitted.
**Junior/Senior/Big League: Admission charge is permitted.**

## XII - AWARDS

(a) Value of awards and material gifts to individual players must be in accordance with the prevailing rules of the High School Athletic Association of the state in which the player participates.

(b) No awards shall be made to players on the basis of comparable skills or accomplishments. **NOTE:** Honor certificates, team pictures, inexpensive medals or pins give adequate recognition and provide lasting mementos from Little League.

## XIII - COMMERCIALIZATION

(a) Exploitation of Little League in any form or for any purpose is prohibited.

(b) Solicitation for fund raising by Little League (Majors) Division, Minor League, Tee Ball, Junior, Senior or Big League players in or out of uniform is prohibited, except for one fund raising project annually under adult supervision.

(c) A reasonable Little League participation fee may be assessed as a parent's obligation to assure the operational continuity of the local Little League. It is recommended that no fee be collected. AT NO TIME SHOULD PAYMENT OF ANY FEE BE A PREREQUISITE FOR PARTICIPATION IN ANY LEVEL OF THE LITTLE LEAGUE PROGRAM. It is recommended that parents who are unable to pay a participation fee be encouraged to contribute volunteer time to the league.

## XIV - FIELD DECORUM

(a) The actions of players, managers, coaches, umpires and league officials must be above reproach. Any player, manager, coach, umpire or league representative who is involved in a verbal or physical altercation, or an incident of unsportsmanlike conduct, at the game site or any other Little League activity, is subject to disciplinary action by the Local League Board of Directors **(or by the district, if the Big League is administered as a district operation)**.

(b) Uniformed players, news photographers, managers, coaches and umpires only shall be permitted within the confines of the playing field just prior to and during games. Batboys and/or batgirls are not permitted at any level of play. Except for the batter, base-runners, and base coaches at first and third bases, all players shall be on their benches in their dugouts or in the bull pen when the team is at bat. When the team is on defense, all reserve players shall be on their benches or in the bullpen.

(c) Two adult base coaches are permitted.

(d) A manager or coach shall not leave the bench or dugout except to confer with a player or an umpire and only after receiving permission from an umpire. (Exception: In Minor League and Tee Ball, managers and coaches may be on the field for instructional purposes, but shall not assist runners or touch a live ball. At least one adult manager or coach must be in the dugout at all times.)

(e) The use of tobacco and alcoholic beverages in any form is prohibited on the playing field, benches or dugouts. Alcohol is prohibited at the game site.

(f) Managers and coaches shall not warm up pitchers.

## XV – APPEARANCE OF LITTLE LEAGUERS IN THE MEDIA

(a) The appearance of Little League players in uniform in advertisements of any kind, or on commercial television programs, or in motion pictures, without the written approval of Little League International, is forbidden.

(b) Brief, televised reports of games and activities on news programs are permitted.

(c) The televising of regular season games, special games, or International Tournament games on a local or regional basis is permitted, provided a contract (available at www.LittleLeague.org) is in place, and provided written permission from Little League Baseball International has been received to televise the specific game(s) or tournament(s).

(d) Radio broadcasts of regular season games and special games are permitted, provided a "Little League Regular Season Radio Contract" (available at www.LittleLeague.org) for the specific game(s) is properly completed and on file with the local league.

(e) Radio broadcasts of International Tournament games are permitted, provided a "Little League International Tournament Radio Contract" (available at www.LittleLeague.org) for the specific game(s) or tournament is properly completed and on file with the district.

(f) Internet web casts of regular season games and special games are permitted, provided a "Little League Regular Season Internet Web Cast Contract" (available at www.LittleLeague.org) for the specific game(s) is properly completed and on file with the local league.

(g) Internet web casts of International Tournament games are permitted, provided a "Little League International Tournament Internet Web Cast Contract" (available at www.LittleLeague.org) for the specific game(s) or tournament is properly completed and on file with the district.

## XVI - USE OF LITTLE LEAGUE NAME AND EMBLEM

Use of the Official Emblem "LL," "LLB" and/or words "Little League," "Little League Baseball," "Little Leaguer," "Senior League, "Big League," "Senior League Baseball," "Big League Baseball," "Challenger Division," etc., (registered under Federal Certificate in U.S. Patent Office), is granted to chartered leagues and cannot be extended by Local Leagues to any other organization for any purpose whatsoever. These marks are protected both by a special Act of Congress and registrations with the United States Patent and Trademark Office. All rights in and to any and all marks of Little League Baseball, Incorporated are reserved.

## XVII - TOURNAMENT PLAY

This regulation applies to the International Tournament, which includes the 9-10 Year Old Division, the 10-11 Year Old Division, the Little League (Majors) Division, the Junior League, Senior League and Big League tournaments.

(a) Tournament team practice or tryouts shall be specified by the Tournament Committee.

(b) The practicing of the league's tournament team against other players in the same division in the same league is permitted providing such practice is done out of uniform.

(c) Tournament rules are published herein.

(d) Unless officially notified to the contrary, each league shall assume full responsibility for expenses incurred in tournament competition.

Diagram No. 1

Diagram showing Tee Ball/Minor League/Little League Baseball field layout.
All dimensions are compulsory unless marked "optional" or "recommended."
**NOTE**: Tee Ball basepaths may be 50 feet.

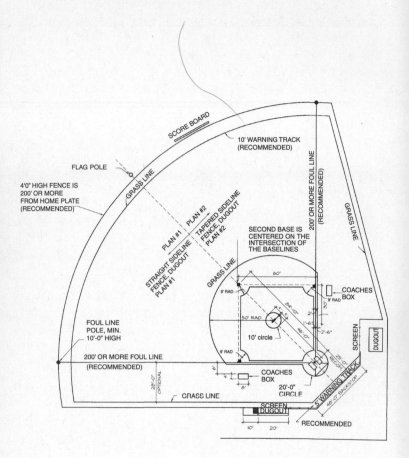

Diagram No. 2
Diagram showing layout of batter's box and compulsory dimensions.

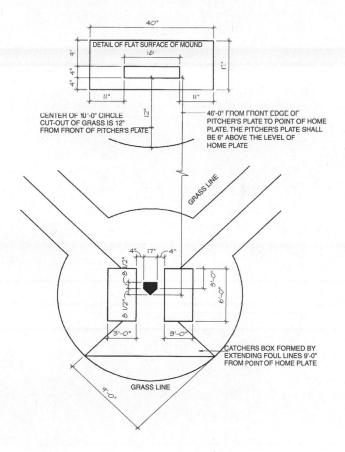

DETAIL OF FLAT SURFACE OF MOUND

40"

9"

4"

4"

18"

11"

11"

12"

CENTER OF 10'-0" CIRCLE
CUT-OUT OF GRASS IS 12"
FROM FRONT OF PITCHER'S PLATE

46'-0" FROM FRONT EDGE OF
PITCHER'S PLATE TO POINT OF HOME
PLATE. THE PITCHER'S PLATE SHALL
BE 6" ABOVE THE LEVEL OF
HOME PLATE

GRASS LINE

4" 17" 4"

8 1/2"

8 1/2"

3'-0"

6'-0"

3'-0"

3'-0"

CATCHERS BOX FORMED BY
EXTENDING FOUL LINES 9'-0"
FROM POINT OF HOME PLATE

GRASS LINE

9'-0"

Diagram No. 3
Diagram showing Junior/Senior/Big League Baseball field layout.
All dimensions are compulsory unless marked "optional" or "recommended."
**NOTE**: Junior basepaths may be 80 feet.

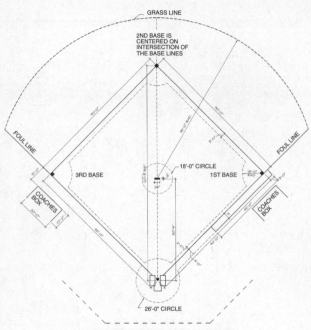

Diagram No. 4
Diagram showing layout of Junior/Senior/Big League Baseball
batter's box and  compulsory dimensions.

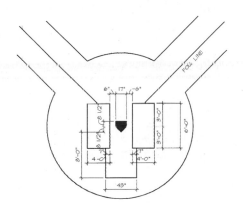

Diagram No. 5

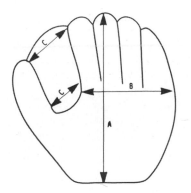

See Rule 1.13, and Rule 1.14

## OFFICIAL PLAYING RULES
## LITTLE LEAGUE BASEBALL (MAJORS) DIVISION, MINOR LEAGUE BASEBALL, TEE BALL BASEBALL, JUNIOR LEAGUE BASEBALL, SENIOR LEAGUE BASEBALL, BIG LEAGUE BASEBALL

### 1.00 - OBJECTIVES OF THE GAME

**1.01** - Little League Baseball in all divisions is a game between two teams of nine players each, under the direction of a manager and not more than two rostered coaches, played on a regulation Little League field in accordance with these rules, under the jurisdiction of one or more umpires. **Tee Ball/Minor League Instructional Division is a game between two teams, under the direction of a manager and not more than two coaches, played on a regulation Little League field in accordance with these rules, under the jurisdiction of one or more umpires. Note: Competitive minor leagues and above may only use nine players on defense. See Rules 4.16 and 4.17.**

**1.02** - The objective of each team is to win by scoring more runs than the opponent. (Tee Ball: It is recommended that no score be kept.)

**1.03** - The winner of the game shall be that team which shall have scored, in accordance with these rules the greater number of runs at the conclusion of a regulation game.

**1.04** - THE PLAYING FIELD. The field shall be laid out according to the instructions, supplemented by Diagrams No. 1 and No. 2 on pages 46 and 47 (Diagrams No. 3 and No. 4 on pages 48 and 49 for **Junior/Senior/Big League Baseball**).

The infield shall be a 60-foot square for Little League Baseball (majors) division, Minor League Baseball and Tee Ball. For **Junior/Senior/Big League Baseball**, the infield shall be a 90-foot square. (Tee Ball option: The infield may be a 50-foot square.)

The outfield shall be the area between the two foul lines formed by extending two sides of the square, as in Diagram 1. The distance from home base to the nearest fence, stand or other obstruction on fair territory should be 200 feet or more (300 feet or more for **Junior/Senior/Big League Baseball**). A distance of 200 feet or more (300 feet or more for **Junior/Senior/Big League Baseball**) along the foul lines, and to center field is recommended. The infield shall be graded so that the base lines and home plate are level.

The pitcher's plate shall be six inches (10 inches for **Junior/Senior/Big League Baseball**) above the level of home plate. The infield and outfield, including the boundary lines, are fair territory and all other area is foul territory.

It is desirable that the line from home base through the pitcher's plate to second base shall run east-northeast.

It is recommended that the distance from home base to the backstop, and from the base lines to the nearest fence, stand or other obstruction on foul territory should be 25 feet or more (45 feet or more for **Junior/Senior/Big League Baseball**). See Diagrams.

When the location of home base is determined, with a steel tape measure 84 feet, 10 inches (127 feet 3 3/8 inches for **Junior/Senior/Big League Baseball**) in the desired direction to establish second base. From home base, measure 60 feet (90 feet for **Junior/Senior/Big League Baseball**) towards first base, from second base, measure 60 feet (90 feet for **Junior/Senior/Big League Baseball**) towards first base; the intersection of these lines establishes first base. From home base, measure 60 feet (90 feet for **Junior/Senior/Big League Baseball**) towards third base; from second base measure 60 feet (90 feet for **Junior/Senior/Big League Baseball**) towards third base; the intersection of these lines establishes third base. The distance between first base and third base is 84 feet, 10 inches (127 feet 3 3/8 inches for **Junior/Senior/Big League Baseball**). All measurements from home base shall be taken from the point where the first and third base lines intersect. (Base paths of 80 feet are optional for **Junior League** regular season play only.)

The catcher's box, the batter's box, the base coaches' boxes and the runner's lane shall be laid out as shown in Diagrams.

The catcher's box extends approximately 6 feet 4-3/4 inches to the rear of home plate. It is determined by extending each foul line 9 feet beyond the back point of home plate. **Junior/Senior/Big League Baseball**: The rear line of the catcher's box is 8 feet directly back from the point of home plate. It extends forward to the rear line of the batter's box. It is 3 feet 7 inches wide.

The batter's box shall be rectangular, 6 feet by 3 feet (6 feet by 4 feet for **Junior/Senior/Big League Baseball**). The inside line, if used, shall be parallel to and 4 inches away (6 inches away for **Junior/Senior/Big League Baseball**) from the side of home plate. It shall extend forward from the center of home plate 3 feet and to the rear 3 feet.

The base coaches' boxes shall be 4 feet by 8 feet (10 feet by 20 feet for **Junior/ Senior/Big League Baseball**) and shall not be closer than 6 feet from (10 feet for **Junior/Senior/Big League Baseball**) the foul lines.

The foul lines and all other playing lines indicated in the diagrams by solid black lines shall be marked with chalk or other white material. Caustic lime must not be used.

The grass lines and dimensions shown on the diagrams are those used in many fields, but they are not mandatory. Each league shall determine the size and shape of the grassed and bare areas of its playing field.

**1.05** - Home base shall be marked by a five-sided slab of whitened rubber. It shall be a 17-inch square with two of the corners filled in so that one edge is 17 inches long, two 8-1/2 inches and two are 12 inches. It shall be set in the ground with the point at the intersection of the lines extending from home base to first base and to third base; with the 17-inch edge facing the pitcher's plate and the two 12-inch edges coinciding with the first and third base lines. The top edges of home base shall be beveled and the base shall be fixed in the ground level with the ground surface. The black beveled edge is not considered part of home plate.

**1.06** - First, second and third bases shall be marked by white canvas or rubber covered bags, securely attached to the ground. The first and third base bags shall be entirely within the infield. The second base bag shall be centered on second base. The base bags shall not be less than fourteen (14) nor more than fifteen (15) inches square and the outer edges shall not be more than two and one-fourth (2¼) inches thick and filled with a soft material. **Leagues are required to ensure that first, second and third bases will disengage their anchor.**

**NOTE 1**: If a base is dislodged from its position during a play, any following runner on the same play shall be considered as touching or occupying the base if, in the umpire's judgment, that runner touches or occupies the dislodged bag or the point marked by the original location of the dislodged bag.

**NOTE 2**: Use of the "Double First Base" is permissible at all levels of play. See Rule 7.15.

**1.07** - The pitcher's plate shall be a rectangular slab of whitened rubber 18 inches by 4 inches (24 inches by 6 inches for **Junior/Senior/Big League Baseball**). It shall be set in the ground as shown in the Diagrams, so that the distance between the front side of the pitcher's plate and home base (the rear point of home plate) shall be 46 feet (60 feet 6 inches for **Junior/Senior/Big League baseball**; **NOTE:** 54 feet pitching distance is optional for **Junior League** regular season only).

**1.08** - The league shall furnish player's benches, one each for the home and visiting teams. Such benches should not be less than twenty-five feet from the base lines. They shall be protected by wire fencing.

**NOTE 1**: The on-deck position is not permitted in Tee Ball, Minor League or Little League (Majors) Division.

**NOTE 2**: Only the first batter of each half-inning will be permitted outside the dugout between half-innings in Tee Ball, Minor League or Little League (Majors) Division.

**1.09** - The ball used must meet Little League specifications and standards. It shall weigh not less than five (5) nor more than five and one-fourth (5-1/4) ounces, and measure not less than nine (9) nor more than nine and one-fourth (9-l/4) inches in circumference. (Tee Ball: The ball may carry the words "Little League Tee Ball.")

**NOTE**: Baseballs licensed by Little League will be printed with one of two designations: "RS" (for regular season play) or "RS-T" (for regular season and tournament play).

**1.10** - The bat must be a baseball bat which meets Little League specifications and standards as noted in this rule. It shall be a smooth, rounded stick and made of wood or of material and color tested and proved acceptable to Little League standards.

**Little League (Majors) and below**: it shall not be more than thirty-three (33) inches in length nor more than two and one-quarter (2¼) inches in diameter. Non-wood bats shall be printed with a BPF (bat performance factor) of 1.15 or less;

**Junior League:** it shall not be more than 34 inches in length; nor more than 2 5/8 inches in diameter, and if wood, not less than fifteen-sixteenths (15/16) inches in diameter (7/8 inch for bats less than 30") at its smallest part.

**Senior/Big League:** it shall not be more than 36 inches in length, nor more than 2 5/8 inches in diameter, and if wood, not less than fifteen-sixteenths (15/16) inches in diameter (7/8 inch for bats less than 30") at its smallest part. The bat shall not weigh, numerically, more than three ounces less than the length of the bat (e.g., a 33-inch-long bat cannot weigh less than 30 ounces). All non-wood bats shall meet the BESR performance standard, and such bats shall be labeled with a permanent certification mark.

In all divisions, wood bats may be taped or fitted with a sleeve for a distance not exceeding sixteen (16) inches (18 inches for Junior/Senior/Big League baseball) from the small end. A non-wood bat must have a grip of cork, tape or composition material, and must extend a minimum of 10 inches from the small end. Slippery tape or similar material is prohibited. An illegal bat must be removed. Any bat that has been altered shall be removed from play.

**NOTE 1: Junior/Senior/Big League:** The 2¾ inch in diameter bat is not allowed in any division.

**NOTE 2:** The traditional batting donut is not permissible

**NOTE 3:** The bat may carry the mark "Little League Tee Ball."

**NOTE 4:** Non-wood bats may develop dents from time to time. Bats that cannot pass through the approved Little League bat ring for the appropriate division must be removed from play. The 2¼ inch bat ring must be used for bats in the Tee Ball, Minor League and Little League Baseball divisions. The 2 5/8 inch bat ring must be used for bats in the Junior, Senior and Big League divisions of baseball.

**1.11** -

(a)  (1)  All players on a team shall wear numbered uniforms identical in color, trim and style.

(2)  The Official Little League Shoulder Patch must be affixed to the upper left sleeve of the uniform blouse. Patches are worn 3" below the left shoulder seam on raglan sleeve; 1" below seam on set-in sleeve; over left breast on sleeveless style.

(3)  Any part of the pitcher's undershirt or T-shirt exposed to view shall be of a solid color. A pitcher shall not wear any items on his/her hands, wrists or arms which may be distracting to the batter. **NOTE:** White long sleeve shirts are not permitted.

(b)  A league must provide each team with a distinctive uniform. Uniforms are the property of the league. Minor League and Tee Ball: T-shirts and caps are recommended, but hand-me-down uniforms may be worn.

(c)  Sleeve lengths may vary for individual players, but the sleeves of each individual shall be approximately the same length. No player shall wear ragged, frayed or slit sleeves.

(d)  No players shall attach to a uniform tape or other material of a different color than the uniform.

(e)  No part of the uniform shall include a pattern that imitates or suggests the shape of a baseball.

(f)  Glass buttons and polished metal shall not be used on a uniform.

(g)  No player shall attach anything to the heel or toe of the shoe other than a toe plate.

(h)  Shoes with metal spikes or cleats are not permitted. Shoes with molded cleats are permissible. (Junior/Senior/Big League: shoes with metal spikes or cleats are permitted.)

(i)  Managers and coaches must not wear conventional baseball uniforms or shoes with metal spikes but may wear cap, slacks and shirt. (**Junior/Senior/Big League**: Managers and coaches may wear conventional baseball uniforms or cap, slacks and shirts. They may not wear shoes with metal spikes.)

(j)  Players must not wear watches, rings, pins, jewelry or other metallic items. (**EXCEPTION**: Jewelry that alerts medical personnel to a specific condition is permissible.)

(k)  Casts may not be worn during the game by players and umpires. **NOTE:** Persons wearing casts, including managers and coaches, must remain in the dugout during the game.

**1.12** - The catcher must wear a catcher's mitt (not a first baseman's mitt or fielder's glove) of any shape, size or weight consistent with protecting the hand.

**1.13** - The first baseman must wear a glove or mitt of any weight with the following maximum specifications:

A – not more than 14 inches long (measured from the bottom edge or heel straight up across the center of the palm to a line even with the highest point of the glove or mitt), and; B – not more than eight inches wide across the palm (measured from the bottom edge of the webbing farthest from the thumb in a horizontal line to the outside of the little finger edge of the glove or mitt), and, C – webbing not more than 5 ¾ inches wide (measured across the top end or along any line parallel to the top). See Diagram No. 5.

**1.14** - Each defensive player (other than the first baseman and catcher) must wear a glove of any weight, with the same maximum specifications as noted in Rule 1.13.

**1.15** -

(a)   The pitcher's glove may not, exclusive of the piping, be white or light gray, nor, in the judgment of an umpire distracting in any manner.

(b)   No pitcher shall attach to the glove any foreign material of a color different from the glove. The pitcher may wear a batting glove on the non-pitching hand under the pitcher's glove provided the batting glove is not white, gray, or optic yellow.

(c)   No pitcher shall wear sweat bands on his/her wrists.

**1.16** - Each league shall provide in the dugout or bench of the offensive team six (6) (seven (7) for **Junior/Senior/Big League Baseball**) protective helmets which must meet NOCSAE specifications and standards. Use of the helmet by the batter, all base runners and base coaches is mandatory. Use of a helmet by an adult base coach is optional. Each helmet shall have an exterior warning label. The helmets provided by each league must meet NOCSAE specifications and bear the NOCSAE stamp as well as an exterior warning label as noted above. **Warning!** Manufacturers have advised that altering helmets in any way can be dangerous. Altering the helmet in any form, including painting or adding decals (by anyone other than the manufacturer or authorized dealer) may void the helmet warranty. Helmets may not be re-painted and may not contain tape or re-applied decals unless approved in writing by the helmet manufacturer or authorized dealer.

**1.17** - All male players must wear athletic supporters. Male catchers must wear the metal, fibre or plastic type cup, and a long-model chest protector. Female catchers must wear long or short model chest protectors. **Junior/Senior/Big League** catchers must wear approved long or short model chest protectors. All catchers must wear chest protectors with neck collar, throat guard, shin guards and catcher's helmet, all of which must meet Little League specifications and standards.The catcher's helmet must meet NOCSAE specifications and standards, and bear the NOCSAE stamp. All catchers must wear a mask, "dangling" type throat protector and catcher's helmet during infield/outfield practice, pitcher warm-up and games. **NOTE**: Skull caps are not permitted. **Warning!** Manufacturers have advised that altering helmets in any way can be dangerous. Altering the helmet in any form, including painting or adding decals (by anyone other than the manufacturer or authorized dealer) may void the helmet warranty. Helmets may not be re-painted and may not contain tape or re-applied decals unless approved in writing by the helmet manufacturer or authorized dealer.

## 2.00 - DEFINITION OF TERMS

(All definitions in Rule 2.00 are listed alphabetically)

**ADJUDGED** is a judgment decision by an umpire.

An **APPEAL** is an act of a fielder in claiming a violation of the rules by the offensive team.

A **BACKSTOP** is the barrier erected behind the catcher in order to allow the catcher to retrieve passed balls easily.

A **BALK** is an illegal act by the pitcher with a runner or runners on base entitling all runners to advance one base (**Junior/Senior/Big League**). A balk is not called in the Little League (Majors) Division, Minor League or Tee Ball. (See Rule 8.05 - Illegal Pitch.)

A **BALL** is a pitch which does not enter the strike zone in flight and is not struck at by the batter. (**NOTE**: If the pitch touches the ground and bounces through the strike zone it is a "ball." If such a pitch touches the batter, the batter shall be awarded first base. If the batter swings at such a pitch and misses, it is a strike. **Junior/Senior/Big League Baseball**: If the batter swings at such a pitch after two strikes, the ball cannot be caught, for the purposes of Rule 6.05 (b) and 6.09 (b). If the batter hits such a pitch, the ensuing action shall be the same as if the batter hit the ball in flight.)

A **BASE** is one of four points which must be touched by a runner in order to score a run; more usually applied to the canvas bags and the rubber plate which mark the base points.

A **BASE COACH** is a team member in uniform or an adult manager and/or coach who is stationed in the base coach's box at first and/or third base to direct the batter and the runners. **Note**: Two (2) adult base coaches are permitted at all levels. The second coach may be 16 years or older. See Rule 4.05 (2) for restrictions.

A **BASE ON BALLS** is an award of first base granted to batters who, during their time at bat, receive four pitches outside the strike zone.

A **BATTER** is an offensive player who takes a position in the batter's box.

**BATTER-RUNNER** is a term that identifies the offensive player who has just finished a time at bat until that player is put out or until the play on which that player becomes a runner ends.

The **BATTER'S BOX** is the area within which the batter must stand during a time at bat.

The **BATTERY** is the pitcher and catcher.

The **BATTING ORDER** is the list of current defensive players (and the designated hitter in Big League) in the order in which they are to bat. **Exceptions**: In all divisions, the batting order may contain the entire roster of players. In Tee Ball, the batting order shall contain the entire roster of players.

**BENCH OR DUGOUT** is the seating facilities reserved for players, substitutes, one manager, and not more than two coaches when they are not actively engaged on the playing field. Batboys and/or batgirls are not permitted.

A **BUNT** is a batted ball not swung at, but intentionally met with the bat and tapped slowly. The mere holding of the bat in the strike zone is not an attempted bunt. (Tee Ball: Bunts are not permitted. Batters are not permitted to take a half-swing. If the umpire feels the batter is taking a half-swing, the batter may be called back to swing again.)

A **CALLED GAME** is one in which, for any reason, the umpire-in-chief terminates play.

A **CATCH** is the act of a fielder in getting secure possession in the hand or glove of a ball in flight and firmly holding it before it touches the ground providing such fielder does not use cap, protector, pocket or any other part of the uniform in getting possession. It is not a catch, however, if simultaneously or immediately following contact with the ball, the fielder collides with a player, or with a wall, or if that fielder falls down, and as a result of such collision or falling, drops the ball. It is not a catch if a fielder touches a fly ball which then hits a member of the offensive team or an umpire and then is caught by another defensive player. If the fielder has made the catch and drops the ball while in the act of making a throw following the catch, the ball shall be adjudged to have been caught. In establishing the validity of the catch, the fielder shall hold the ball long enough to prove complete control of the ball and that release of the ball is voluntary and intentional. A catch is legal if the ball is finally held by any fielder, even though juggled, or held by another fielder before it touches the ground. Runners may leave their bases the instant the first fielder touches the ball.

The **CATCHER** is the fielder who takes the position back of the home base.

The **CATCHER'S BOX** is that area within which the catcher shall stand until the pitcher delivers the ball. (See Rule 4.03)

A **COACH** is an adult appointed to perform such duties as the manager may designate. **NOTE:** If two (2) coaches are appointed, the second coach may be age 16 or older.

A **DEAD BALL** is a ball out of play because of a legally created temporary suspension of play.

The **DEFENSE** (or **DEFENSIVE**) is the team, or any player of the team, in the field.

A **DOUBLE HEADER** is two regularly scheduled or rescheduled games, played by the same team(s) on the same day.

A **DOUBLE PLAY** is a play by the defense in which two offensive players are put out as a result of continuous action, providing there is no error between putouts.

(a) A force double play is one in which both putouts are force plays.

(b) A reverse force double play is one in which the first out is made at any base and the second out is made by tagging a runner who originally was forced, before the runner touches the base to which that runner was forced.

**DUGOUT** (see definition of "BENCH")

A **FAIR BALL** is a batted ball that settles on fair ground between home and first base, or between home and third base, or that is on or over fair territory when bounding to the outfield past first or third base, or that touches first, second or third base, or that first falls on fair territory on or beyond first base or third base, or that, while on or over fair territory touches the person of an umpire or player, or that, while over fair territory, passes out of the playing field in flight.

**NOTE**: A fair fly shall be adjudged according to the relative position of the ball and the foul line, including the foul pole, and not as to whether the fielder is on fair or foul territory at the time such fielder touches the ball.

**FAIR TERRITORY** is that part of the playing field within, and including the first base and third base lines, from home base to the bottom of the playing field fence and perpendicularly upwards. Home plate, first base and third base and all foul lines are in fair territory.

A **FIELDER** is any defensive player.

**FIELDER'S CHOICE** is the act of a fielder who handles a fair grounder and, instead of throwing it to first base to put out the batter-runner, throws to another base in an attempt to put out a preceding runner. The term is also used by scorers (a) to account for the advance of the batter-runner who takes one or more extra bases when the fielder who handles the safe hit attempts to put out a preceding runner; (b) to account for the advance of a runner (other than by stolen base or error) while a fielder is attempting to put out another runner; and (c) to account for the advance of a runner made solely because of the defensive team's indifference. (Undefended steal).

A **FLY BALL** is a batted ball that goes high in the air in flight.

A **FORCE PLAY** is a play in which a runner legally loses the right to occupy a base by reason of the batter becoming a runner. (**NOTE**: Confusion regarding this play is removed by remembering that frequently the "force" situation is removed during the play. Example: Runner on first, one out, ground ball hit sharply to first baseman, who touches the base and the batter runner is out. The force is removed at that moment and the runner advancing to second must be tagged. If there had been a runner at second or third, and either of these runners scored before the tag-out at second, the run(s) would count. Had the first baseman thrown to second and the ball had been returned to first, the play at second would have been a force-out, making two outs, and the return throw to first would have made the third out. In that case, no run would score.)

A **FORFEITED GAME** is a game declared ended by the umpire-in-chief in favor of the offended team by the score of 6 to 0 (7-0 for Junior/Senior/Big League), for violation of the rules. (Tee Ball: There shall be no forfeits in Tee Ball.)

A **FOUL BALL** is a batted ball that settles on foul territory between home and first base, or between home and third base, or that bounds past first or third base on or over foul territory, or that first falls on foul territory beyond first or third base, or that while on or over foul territory, touches the person of an umpire or player, or any object foreign to the natural ground.

**NOTE (1)**: A foul fly shall be judged according to the relative position of the ball and the foul line, including the foul pole, and not as to whether the fielder is on foul or fair territory at the time that fielder touches the ball.

**NOTE (2)**: In Tee Ball, the ball is foul if it travels less than 15 feet in fair territory from home plate. The ball is also foul if the batter hits the tee with the bat.

**FOUL TERRITORY** is that part of the playing field outside the first and third base lines extended to the fence and perpendicularly upwards.

A **FOUL TIP** is a batted ball that goes sharp and direct from the bat to the catcher's hands and is legally caught. It is not a foul tip unless caught and any foul tip that is caught is a strike, and the ball is in play. It is not a catch if it is a rebound, unless the ball has first touched the catcher's glove or hand. A foul tip can only be caught by the catcher.

A **GROUND BALL** is a batted ball that rolls or bounces close to the ground.

The **HOME TEAM** is the team which takes the field first at the start of the game. Adopted schedules will determine which team this will be.

**ILLEGAL** (or ILLEGALLY) is contrary to these rules.

An **ILLEGAL PITCH** is (1) a pitch delivered to the batter when the pitcher does not have the pivot foot in contact with the pitcher's plate; (2) a quick return pitch, or any other act meeting the criteria established in Rule 8.05. Junior/Senior/Big League: An illegal pitch with runners on base is a balk. (See also "Pitch")

An **ILLEGALLY BATTED BALL** is one hit by the batter with one or both feet on the ground entirely outside the batter's box.

**INELIGIBLE PITCHER** - Applies to regular season violations of Regulation VI. (See also Rule 4.19.)

**INELIGIBLE PLAYER** - Applies to regular season violations of regulations regarding league age, residence (as defined by Little League Baseball, Incorporated) and participation on the proper team within the Local League. (See also Rule 4.19.)

The **INFIELD** is that portion of the field in fair territory, which includes areas normally covered by infielders.

An **INFIELDER** is a fielder who occupies a position in the infield.

An **INFIELD FLY** is a fair fly ball (not including a line drive nor an attempted bunt) which can be caught by an infielder with ordinary effort, when first and second, or first, second and third bases are occupied, before two are out. The pitcher, catcher and any outfielder stationed in the infield on the play shall be considered infielders for the purpose of this rule.

When it seems apparent that a batted ball will be an Infield Fly, the umpire shall immediately declare "Infield Fly" for the benefit of the runners. If the ball is near the baseline, the umpire shall declare "Infield Fly if Fair."

The ball is alive and runners may advance at the risk of that ball being caught, or retouch and advance after the ball is touched, the same as on any fly ball. If the hit becomes a foul ball, it is treated the same as any foul.

**NOTE (1):** If a declared Infield Fly is allowed to fall untouched to the ground, and bounces foul and remains foul before passing first or third base, it is a foul ball. If a declared Infield Fly falls untouched to the ground, outside the baseline, and bounces fair before passing first or third base, it is an Infield Fly.

**NOTE (2):** The Infield Fly Rule does not apply in Tee Ball.

**IN FLIGHT** describes a batted, thrown, or pitched ball which has not yet touched the ground or some object other than a fielder. If the pitch touches the ground and bounces through the strike zone, without being struck at by the batter, it is a "ball." If such a pitch touches the batter, that batter shall be awarded first base. **Junior/Senior/Big League** - If the batter swings at such a pitch after two strikes, the ball cannot be caught for the purpose of Rule 6.05 (b)**.** If the batter hits such a pitch, the ensuing action shall be the same as if the ball was hit in flight.

**IN JEOPARDY** is a term indicating that the ball is in play and an offensive player may be put out.

An **INNING** is that portion of a game within which the teams alternate on offense and defense and in which there are three putouts for each team. Each team's time at bat is a half-inning. It will be held that an inning starts the moment the third out is made completing the preceding inning. **(Minor League Only – A five-run limit is to be imposed, which would complete the half inning.)**

## INTERFERENCE

(a) Offensive interference is an act by a member of the team at bat which interferes with, obstructs, impedes, hinders or confuses any fielder attempting to make a play. If the umpire declares the batter, batter-runner or a runner out for interference, all other runners shall return to the last base that was, in the judgment of the umpire, legally touched at the time of the interference, unless otherwise provided by these rules.

(b) Defensive interference is an act by a fielder which hinders or prevents a batter from hitting a pitch.

(c) Umpire's interference occurs (1) when an umpire hinders, impedes or prevents a catcher's throw attempting to prevent a stolen base, or (2) when a fair ball touches an umpire on fair territory before passing a fielder.

(d) Spectator interference occurs when a spectator reaches out of the stands or goes on the playing field, and touches a live ball.

(e) On any interference the ball is dead.

The **LEAGUE** is a group of teams who play each other in a pre-arranged schedule under these rules for the league championship.

**LEGAL** (or **LEGALLY**) is in accordance with these rules.

A **LINE DRIVE** is a batted ball that goes sharp and direct from the bat to a fielder without touching the ground.

A **LIVE BALL** is a ball which is in play.

The **MANAGER** is an adult appointed by the president to be responsible for the team's actions on the field, and to represent the team in communications with the umpire and the opposing team.

(a) The manager shall always be responsible for the team's conduct, observance of the official rules and deference to the umpires.

(b) If a manager leaves the field, that manager shall designate an adult coach as a substitute and such substitute manager shall have the duties, rights and responsibilities of the manager. If no adult coach is available, the umpire-in-chief shall designate a temporary adult manager. If no adult is available, the game or team activities shall be terminated. (See Rule 4.16.)

**OBSTRUCTION** is the act of a fielder who, while not in possession of the ball, impedes the progress of any runner. A fake tag is considered obstruction. (**NOTE**: Obstruction shall be called on a defensive player who blocks off a base, base line or home plate from a base runner while not in possession of the ball.)

**OFFENSE** is the team, or any player of the team, at bat.

**OFFICIAL RULES**. The rules contained in this book.

**OFFICIAL SCORER**. See Rule 10.00 in "What's the Score" publication.

An **OUT** is one of the three required retirements of an offensive team during its time at bat.

The **OUTFIELD** is that portion of the field in fair territory which is normally covered by outfielders.

An **OUTFIELDER** is a fielder who occupies a position in the outfield, which is the area of the playing field most distant from home base.

**OVERSLIDE** (or OVERSLIDING) is the act of an offensive player when the slide to a base, other than when advancing from home to first base, is with such momentum that the player loses contact with the base.

A **PENALTY** is the application of these rules following an illegal act.

The **PERSON** of a player or an umpire is any part of the body, clothing or equipment.

A **PITCH** is a ball delivered to the batter by the pitcher. Exception: For the purpose of maintaining a pitch count, a balk or illegal pitch shall count as one pitch; even if a pitch is not actually thrown.

A **PITCHER** is the fielder designated to deliver the pitch to the batter.

The Pitcher's **PIVOT FOOT** is that foot which is in contact with the pitcher's plate as the pitch is delivered.

"**PLAY**" is the umpire's order to start the game or to resume action following any dead ball.

A **QUICK RETURN** is a pitch made with obvious intent to catch a batter off balance. It is an illegal pitch. (See Penalty – 8.05)

**REGULATION GAME**. See Rules 4.10 and 4.11.

A **RETOUCH** is the act of a runner returning to a base as legally required.

A **RUN** (or **SCORE**) is the score made by an offensive player who advances from batter to runner and touches first, second, third and home bases in that order.

A **RUNDOWN** is the act of the defense in an attempt to put out a runner between bases.

A **RUNNER** is an offensive player who is advancing toward, or touching, or returning to any base.

"**SAFE**" is a declaration by the umpire that a runner is entitled to the base for which that runner was trying.

**SET POSITION** is one of the two legal pitching positions.

A **STRIKE** is a legal pitch which meets any of these conditions -

    (a)   is struck at by the batter and is missed;

    (b)   is not struck at, if any part of the ball passes through any part of the strike zone;

    (c)   is fouled by the batter when there is less than two strikes;

    (d)   is bunted foul (batter is out and ball is dead, if the batter bunts foul on the third strike);

    (e)   touches the batter's person as the batter strikes at it (dead ball);

    (f)   touches the batter in flight in the strike zone; or

    (g)   becomes a foul tip (ball is live and in play).

**NOTE**: In Tee Ball, the Local League will determine whether or not strikeouts will be permitted.

The **STRIKE ZONE** is that space over home plate which is between the batter's armpits and the top of the knees when the batter assumes a natural stance. The umpire shall determine the strike zone according to the batter's usual stance when that batter swings at a pitch.

A **SUSPENDED GAME** is a called game which is to be completed at a later date.

A **TAG** is the action of a fielder in touching a base with the body while holding the ball securely and firmly in the hand or glove; or touching a runner with the ball or with the hand or glove holding the ball, while holding the ball securely and firmly in the hand or glove.

A **THROW** is the act of propelling the ball with the hand and arm to a given objective and is to be always distinguished from the pitch.

A **TIE GAME** is a regulation game which is called when each team has the same number of runs.

"**TIME**" is the announcement by the umpire of a legal interruption of play, during which the ball is dead.

**TOUCH**. To touch a player or umpire is to touch any part of the player or umpire's body, clothing or equipment.

A **TRIPLE PLAY** is a play by the defense in which three offensive players are put out as a result of continuous action, providing there is no error between putouts.

A **WILD PITCH** is one so high, or low, or wide of the plate that it cannot be handled with ordinary effort by the catcher.

**WIND-UP-POSITION** is one of the two legal pitching positions.

### 3.00 - GAME PRELIMINARIES

**3.01** - Before the game begins the umpires shall-

    (a) require strict observance of all rules governing team personnel, implements of play and equipment of players;

    (b) be sure that all playing lines (heavy lines on Diagrams No. 1 and No. 2) are marked with non-caustic lime, chalk or other white material easily distinguishable from the ground or grass;

    (c) receive from the league a supply of baseballs which meet Little League specifications and standards; The umpire shall be the sole judge of the fitness of the balls to be used in the game;

    (d) be assured by the league that additional balls are immediately available for use if required;

    (e) have possession of at least two alternate balls and shall require replenishment of such supply of alternate balls as needed throughout the game. Such alternate balls shall be put in play when -

        (1) a ball has been batted out of the playing field or into the spectator area;

        (2) a ball has become discolored or unfit for further use;

        (3) the pitcher requests such alternate ball.

**3.02** - No player shall intentionally discolor or damage the ball by rubbing it with soil, rosin, paraffin, licorice, sandpaper, emery-paper or other foreign substance.

**PENALTY**: The umpire shall demand the ball and remove the offender from the pitching position. In case the umpire cannot locate the offender, and if the pitcher delivers such discolored or damaged ball to the batter, the pitcher shall be removed from the pitching position at once.

**3.03** - A player in the starting line-up who has been removed for a substitute may re-enter the game once, in any position in the batting order, provided:

    1. his or her substitute has completed one time at bat and;

    2. has played defensively for a minimum of six (6) consecutive outs;

    3. pitchers once removed from the mound may not return as pitchers; **Junior/Senior/Big League** - A pitcher remaining in the game, but moving to a different position, can return as a pitcher any time in the remainder of the game, but only once per game.

    4. only a player in the starting line-up may re-enter the game;

    5. a starter, (S1) re-entering the game as a substitute for another starter (S2) must then fulfill all conditions of a substitute (once at bat and six defensive outs) before starter (S2) can re-enter the game.

6.   Defensive substitutions must be made while the team is on defense. Offensive substitutions must be made at the time the offensive player has her/his turn at bat or is on base.

**NOTE 1**: A substitute may not be removed from the game prior to completion of his/her mandatory play requirements.

**NOTE 2:** When two or more substitute players of the defensive team enter the game at the same time, the manager shall, immediately before they take their positions as fielders, designate to the umpire-in-chief such player's positions in the team's batting order and the umpire-in-chief shall notify the official scorer. The umpire-in-chief shall have authority to designate the substitute's places in the batting order, if this information is not immediately provided.

**NOTE 3:** If during a game either team is unable to place nine (9) players on the field due to illness, injury or ejection, the opposing manager shall select a player previously used in the lineup to re-enter the game, but only if use of all eligible players has exhausted the roster. A player ejected from the game is not eligible for re-entry.

### 3.03 - Big League

(a)   Any player in the starting line-up, including the designated hitter, who has been removed for a substitute may re-enter the game once, provided such player occupies the same batting position as he or she did in the starting lineup.

(b)   A pitcher, withdrawn for a substitute, may not re-enter the game as a pitcher. (**EXCEPTION**: A pitcher may re-enter the game as a pitcher, if withdrawn for a pinch-hitter or pinch-runner, and then returned to the game at the beginning of the next half-inning.)

(c)   A pitcher remaining in the game, but moving to a different position, can return as a pitcher anytime in the remainder of the game, but only once per game.

(d)   Defensive substitutions must be made while the team is on defense. Offensive substitutions must be made at the time the offensive player has her/his turn at bat or is on base.

**Big League Designated Hitter Rule:**

1.   At the beginning of a game, each manager may list on the lineup card a designated hitter to bat throughout the game for a designated player in the regular lineup.

2.   Only a player not in the regular batting order may be used as a designated hitter.

3.   In the event a manager decides to use the designated hitter as a defensive player, the player must remain in the same position in the batting order, unless otherwise replaced by a substitute. If so, the player for whom the designated hitter was batting must be removed from the game. Such player may re-enter the game once, but only in the batting order position of the former designated hitter, who must be removed.

4.   This rule does not change the regular rule governing the use of pinch-hitters.

**3.04** - A player whose name is on the team's batting order may not become a substitute runner for another member of the team. "Courtesy runner" not permitted.

**3.05** -

(a) The pitcher named in the batting order handed to the umpire-in-chief, as provided in Rules 4.01 (a) and 4.01 (b) shall pitch to the first batter or any substitute batter until such batter or any substitute batter is put out or reaches first base, unless the pitcher sustains an injury or illness which, in the judgment of the umpire-in-chief, incapacitates the pitcher from further play as a pitcher.

(b) If the pitcher is replaced, the substitute pitcher shall pitch to the batter then at bat, or any substitute batter, until such batter is put out or reaches first base, or until the offensive team is put out, unless the substitute pitcher sustains an injury or illness, which in the umpire-in-chief's judgment, incapacitates the pitcher from further play as a pitcher.

**3.06** - The manager shall immediately notify the umpire-in-chief of any substitution and shall state to the umpire-in-chief the substitute's place in the batting order.

**3.07** - The umpire-in-chief, after having been notified, shall immediately announce, or cause to be announced, each substitution.

**3.08** -

(a) If no announcement of a substitution is made, the substitute shall be considered to have entered the game when -

  (1) if a pitcher, the substitute takes a position on the pitcher's plate and throws one warm-up pitch to the catcher;

  (2) if a batter, the substitute takes a position in the batter's box;

  (3) if a fielder, the substitute reaches the position usually occupied by the fielder being replaced and play commences;

  (4) if a runner, the substitute takes the place of the runner being replaced.

(b) Any play made by, or on, any of the above mentioned unannounced substitutes shall be legal.

**3.09** - Players, managers and coaches of the participating teams shall not address, or mingle with spectators, nor sit in the stands during a game in which they are engaged. Managers or coaches must not warm up a pitcher at home plate or in the bull pen or elsewhere at any time, They may, however, stand by to observe a pitcher during warm-up in the bullpen.

**3.10** -

(a) The managers of both teams shall agree on the fitness of the playing field before the game starts. In the event that the two managers cannot agree, the president or a duly delegated representative shall make the determination.

(b) The umpire-in chief shall be the sole judge as to whether and when play shall be suspended during a game because of unsuitable weather conditions or the unfit condition of the playing field; as to whether and when play shall be resumed after such suspension; and as to whether and when a game shall be terminated after such suspension. Said umpire shall not call the game until at least thirty minutes after play has been suspended. The umpire may continue suspension as long as there is any chance to resume play.

**3.11** - **Double Headers**

**Little League (Majors) Division**: A team may play one (1) doubleheader in a calendar week. No team shall play three games in a day. (Exception under condition of Rule 4.12.)

**Minor League and Tee Ball**: No team shall be scheduled to play two games in one day. (See Rule 4.12).

**Junior/Senior/Big League**: Doubleheaders are permitted.

**3.12** - When the umpire suspends play, "Time" shall be called. At the umpire's call of "Play" the suspension is lifted and play resumes. Between the call of "Time" and the call of "Play" the ball is dead.

**3.13** - The Local League will establish ground rules to be followed by all teams in the league.

**3.14** - Members of the offensive team shall carry all gloves and other equipment off the field and to the dugout while their team is at bat. No equipment shall be left lying on the field, either in fair or foul territory.

**3.15** - No person shall be allowed on the playing field during a game except uniformed players, managers and coaches, umpires and news photographers authorized by the league. In case of intentional interference with play by any person authorized to be on the playing field, the ball is dead at the moment of the interference and no runners on base may advance. Should an overthrown ball accidentally touch an authorized person, it will not be considered interference and the ball will remain live.

**3.16** - When there is spectator interference with any thrown or batted ball, the ball shall be dead at the moment of interference and the umpire shall impose such penalties as in the umpire's opinion will nullify the act of interference.

**APPROVED RULING**: If spectator interference clearly prevents a fielder from catching a fly ball, the umpire shall declare the batter out.

**3.17** - Players and substitutes shall sit on their team's bench or in the dugout unless participating in the game or preparing to enter the game.

No one except eligible players in uniform, a manager and not more than two coaches shall occupy the bench or dugout. When batters or base runners are retired, they must return to the bench or dugout at once. Batboys and/or batgirls are not permitted. The use of electronic equipment during the game is restricted. No team shall use electronic equipment, including walkie-talkies, cellular telephones, etc., for any communication with on-field personnel including those in the dugout, bullpen or field.

**NOTE**: In Tee Ball and non-competitive Minor Leagues, all players on the roster may be given a defensive position. Only one player may occupy the catcher's position in Tee Ball.

**3.18** - The Local League shall provide proper protection sufficient to preserve order and to prevent spectators from entering the field. Either team may refuse to play until the field is cleared.

## 4.00 - STARTING AND ENDING THE GAME

**4.01** - The umpires shall proceed directly to home plate where they shall be met by the managers of the opposing teams, just preceding the established time to begin the game. In sequence-

(a) the home team manager shall give the batting order in duplicate to the umpire-in-chief;

(b) next, the visiting manager shall give the batting order in duplicate to the umpire-in-chief;

(c) the umpire-in-chief shall make certain that the original and duplicate copies are the same, then provide a copy of each batting order to the opposing manager. The original copy retained by the umpire shall be the official batting order;

(d) as soon as the home team's batting order is handed to the umpire-in-chief, the umpires are in charge of the playing field and from that moment have sole authority to determine when a game shall be called, halted or resumed on account of weather or the conditions of the playing field.

**NOTE**: Rostered players who arrive at the game site after a game begins may be inserted in the lineup, if the manager so chooses. This applies even when a suspended game is resumed at a later date.

**4.02** - The players of the home team shall take their defensive positions, the first batter of the visiting team shall take a position in the batter's box, the umpire shall call "Play" and the game shall start.

**4.03** - When the ball is put in play at the start of, or during a game, all fielders other than the catcher shall be in fair territory.

(a) The catcher shall be stationed in the catcher's box. The catcher may leave that position at any time to catch a pitch or make a play except that when the batter is being given an intentional base on balls, the catcher must stand with both feet within the lines of the catcher's box until the ball leaves the pitcher's hand.

**PENALTY**: Illegal pitch - ball called on the batter (see Rule 8.05). (**Junior/Senior/Big League penalty**: Balk with runner or runners on base.)

(b) The pitcher, while in the act of delivering the ball to the batter, shall take the legal position.

(c) Except the pitcher and the catcher, any fielder may be stationed anywhere in fair territory.

**4.04** - The batting order shall be followed throughout the game unless a player is substituted for another. Substitutes must take the place of the replaced player's position in the batting order except as covered by Rule 3.03. A league may adopt a policy of a continuous batting order that will include all players on the team roster present for the game batting in order. If this option is adopted, each player would be required to bat in his/her respective spot in the batting order. However, a player may be entered and/or re-entered defensively in the game anytime provided he/she meets the requirements of mandatory play. **NOTE 1**: The continuous batting order is mandatory for all Tee Ball and Minor League Divisions. **NOTE 2**: For the Tee Ball and Minor League Division (and when the continuous batting order is adopted for other divisions), when a child is injured, becomes ill or must leave the game site after the start of the game, the team will skip over him/her when his/her time at bat comes up without penalty. If the injured, ill or absent player returns he/she is merely inserted into their original spot in the batting order and the game continues. Also, if a child arrives late to a game site, if the manager chooses to enter him/her in the lineup (see Rule 4.01 **NOTE**), he/she would be added to the end of the current lineup.

**4.05** - The offensive team shall station two base coaches on the field during its time at bat, one near first base and one near third base. The coaches shall not leave their respective dugouts until the pitcher has completed his/her preparatory pitches to the catcher. Base coaches shall-

(1)   be eligible players in the uniform of their team; a manager and/or coach. Both base coaches may be managers or coaches.

(2)   be a manager or coach only if there is at least one other adult manager or coach in the dugout.

(3)   remain within the base coaches' boxes at all times, except as provided in Rule 7.11;

(4)    talk to members of their own team only.

An offending base coach shall be removed from the base coach's box.

**4.06** - No manager, coach or player, shall at any time, whether from the bench or the playing field or elsewhere -

(1)   incite, or try to incite, by word or sign, a demonstration by spectators;

(2)   use language which will in any manner refer to or reflect upon opposing players, manager, coach, an umpire or spectators;

(3)   make any move calculated to cause the pitcher to commit an illegal pitch (a balk in **Junior/Senior/Big League**);

(4)   take a position in the batter's line of vision, with the deliberate intent to distract the batter.

The umpire may first warn the player, coach and/or manager. If continued, remove the player, coach and/or manager from the game or bench. If such action causes an illegal pitch (a balk in **Junior/Senior/Big League**), it shall be nullified.

**4.07** - When a manager, coach or player is ejected from a game, they shall leave the field immediately and take no further part in that game. They may not sit in the stands and may not be recalled. **A manager or coach ejected from a game must not be present at the game site for the remainder of that game.** Any manager, coach or player ejected from a game is suspended for his or her team's next physically played game and may not be in attendance at the game site from which they were suspended.

**4.08** - When the occupants of a player's bench show violent disapproval of an umpire's decision, the umpire shall first give warning that such disapproval shall cease. If such action continues -

**PENALTY**: The umpire shall order the offender out of the game and away from the spectators' area. If the umpire is unable to detect the offender or offenders, the bench may be cleared of all players. The manager of the offending team shall have the privilege of recalling to the playing field only those players needed for substitution in the game.

**4.09** - **HOW A TEAM SCORES**

(a)   One run shall be scored each time a runner legally advances to and touches first, second, third and home base before three players are put out to end the inning.

**EXCEPTIONS**: A run is not scored if the runner advances to home base during a play in which the third out is made (1) by the batter-runner before touching first base; (2) by any runner being forced out; or (3) by a preceding runner who is declared out because that runner failed to touch one of the bases (appeal play).

**APPROVED RULING**: One out, Jones on third, Smith on first and Brown flies out to right field for the second out. Jones tags up and scores after the catch. Smith attempted to return to first but the right fielder's throw beat Smith to the base for the third out. But Jones scored before the throw to catch Smith reached first base. Hence, Jones' run counts. It was not a force play.

(b) When the winning run is scored in the last half-inning of a regulation game, or in the last half of an extra inning, as the result of a base on balls, hit batter or any other play with the bases full which forces the runner on third to advance, the umpire shall not declare the game ended until the runner forced to advance from third has touched home base and the batter-runner has touched first base.

**4.10** -

(a) A regulation game consists of six innings (**Junior/Senior/Big League** - seven innings), unless extended because of a tie score, or shortened (1) because the home team needs none of its half of the sixth inning (**Junior/Senior/Big League** - seventh) or only a fraction of it; or (2) because the umpire calls the game.

(b) If the score is tied after six complete innings (**Junior/Senior/Big League** - seven innings), play shall continue until (1) the visiting team has scored more total runs than the home team at the end of a completed inning; or (2) the home team scores the winning run in an uncompleted inning.

(c) If a game is called, it is a regulation game -
   (1) if four innings have been completed (**Junior/Senior/Big League** - five innings);
   (2) if the home team has scored more runs in three and a half innings than the visiting team has scored in four completed half-innings; (**Junior/Senior/Big League** - four and a half innings)
   (3) if the home team scores one or more runs in its half of the fourth inning (Junior/Senior/Big League - fifth inning) to tie the score.

(d) If a game is called before it has become a regulation game, but after one (1) or more innings have been played, it shall be resumed exactly where it left off. **NOTE**: All records, including pitching, shall be counted.

(e) If after four (4) innings (**Junior/Senior/Big League** - five innings), three and one-half innings (**Junior/Senior/Big League** - four and one-half innings) if the home team is ahead, one team has a lead of ten (10) runs or more, the manager of the team with the least runs shall concede the victory to the opponent. **NOTE**: (1) If the visiting team has a lead of ten (10) runs or more, the home team must bat in its half of the inning. (2) The Local League may adopt the option of not utilizing this rule.

(f) **Tee Ball**: The Local League may determine appropriate game length but shall not exceed 6 innings. It is recommended that Tee Ball games be 4 innings or 1-1/2 hour time limit.

**4.11** - The score of a regulation game is the total number of runs scored by each team at the moment the game ends.

(a)  The game ends when the visiting team completes its half of the sixth inning (**Junior/Senior/Big League** - seventh inning) if the home team is ahead.

(b)  The game ends when the sixth inning (**Junior/Senior/Big League** - seventh inning) is completed, if the visiting team is ahead.

(c)  If the home team scores the winning run in its half of the sixth inning (**Junior/Senior/Big League** - seventh inning), or its half of an extra inning after a tie, the game ends immediately when the winning run is scored.

**NOTE**: Once a game becomes regulation and it is called with the home team taking the lead in an incomplete inning, the game ends with the home team the winner.

**EXCEPTION**: If the last batter in a game hits a home run out of the playing field, the batter-runner and all runners on base are permitted to score, in accordance with the base-running rules, and the game ends when the batter-runner touches home plate.

**APPROVED RULING**: The batter hits a home run out of the playing field to win the game in the last half of the sixth (**Junior/Senior/Big League** - seventh inning) or an extra inning, but is called out for passing a preceding runner. The game ends immediately when the winning run is scored.

(d)  A called game ends at the moment the umpire terminates play.

**EXCEPTION**: If the game is called during an incomplete inning, the game ends at the end of the last previous completed inning in each of the following situations:

(1)  The visiting team scores one or more runs to tie the score in the incomplete inning, and the home team does not score in the incomplete inning.

(2)  The visiting team scores one or more runs to take the lead in the incomplete inning, and the home team does not tie the score or retake the lead in the incomplete inning

(e)  A regulation game that is tied after four (**Junior/Senior/Big League** - five) or more completed innings and halted by the umpire, shall be resumed from the exact point that play was halted. The game shall continue in accordance with Rule 4.10 (a) and 4.10 (b).

**NOTE**: When a TIE game is halted, the pitcher of record may continue pitching in the same game on any subsequent date provided said pitcher has observed the required days of rest for his/her particular age group. For scorekeeping purposes, it shall be considered the same game, and all batting, fielding and pitching records will count.

**LITTLE LEAGUE/MINOR LEAGUE EXAMPLE:**

Rule 4.11

|          | 1 | 2 | 3 | 4 | 5 | 6 |
|----------|---|---|---|---|---|---|
| VISITORS | 0 | 0 | 0 | 4 | 1 |   |
| HOME     | 0 | 0 | 0 | 5 |   |   |

Game called in top of 5th inning on account of rain. Score reverts to last completed inning (4th) and the home team is the winner 5 to 4.

### JUNIOR/SENIOR/BIG LEAGUE EXAMPLE:
Rule 4.11

|          | 1 | 2 | 3 | 4 | 5 | 6 |
|----------|---|---|---|---|---|---|
| VISITORS | 0 | 0 | 0 | 0 | 4 | 1 |
| HOME     | 0 | 0 | 0 | 0 | 5 |   |

Game called in top of 6th inning on account of rain. Score reverts to last completed inning (5th) and the home team is the winner 5 to 4.

**4.12** - TIE games halted due to weather, curfew or light failure shall be resumed from the exact point at which they were halted in the original game.  It can be completed preceding the next scheduled game between the same teams.  **A player may not pitch in more than one game in a day. (EXCEPTION: In the Big League Division a player may be used as a pitcher in up to two games in a day. See Regulation VI.)**  The lineup and batting order of both teams shall be the same as the lineup and batting order at the moment the game was halted, subject to the rules governing substitution.  Any player may be replaced by a player who was not in the game prior to halting the original game.  No player once removed before the game was halted may be returned to the lineup unless covered by Rule 3.03.  NOTE: When a TIE game is halted, the pitcher of record may continue pitching in the same game on any subsequent date provided said pitcher has observed the required days of rest for his/her particular age group. For scorekeeping purposes, it shall be considered the same game, and all batting fielding and pitching records will count.

### LITTLE LEAGUE/MINOR LEAGUE EXAMPLE:
Rule 4.12

Tie games halted due to weather, curfew or light failure shall be resumed from the exact point at which they were halted in the original game.

|          | 1 | 2 | 3 | 4 | 5 | 6 |
|----------|---|---|---|---|---|---|
| VISITORS | 0 | 0 | 0 | 0 | 4 | 5 |
| HOME     | 0 | 0 | 0 | 0 | 4 |   |

Game called in top of 6th inning, visiting team batting with two out, no base runners - this is a tie game. Resume the game in the top of the 6th, visiting team at bat, two out.

### JUNIOR/SENIOR/BIG LEAGUE EXAMPLE:
Rule 4.12

Tie games halted due to weather, curfew or light failure shall be resumed from the exact point at which they were halted in the original game.

|          | 1 | 2 | 3 | 4 | 5 | 6 | 7 |
|----------|---|---|---|---|---|---|---|
| VISITORS | 0 | 0 | 0 | 0 | 0 | 4 | 5 |
| HOME     | 0 | 0 | 0 | 0 | 0 | 4 |   |

Game called in top of 7th inning, visiting team batting with two out, no base runners - this is a tie game. Resume the game in the top of the 7th, visiting team at bat, two out.

**4.13** - Double Headers
**Little League (Majors) Division**: A team may play one (1) doubleheader in a

calendar week. No team shall play three games in a day. (Exception under condition of Rule 4.12.)

**Minor League and Tee Ball**: No team shall be scheduled to play two games in one day. (See Rule 4.12).

**Junior/Senior/Big League**: Doubleheaders are permitted.

**4.14** - The umpire-in-chief shall order the playing field lights turned on whenever in such umpire's opinion that darkness makes further play in daylight hazardous.

**4.15** - A game may be forfeited by the umpire-in-chief of the game in progress to the opposing team when a team -

    (1)   being upon the field, refuses to start play within 10 minutes after the appointed hour for beginning the game, unless such delay, in the umpire's judgment, is unavoidable;

    (2)   refuses to continue play unless the game was terminated by the umpire;

    (3)   fails to resume play, after the game was halted by the umpire, within one minute after the umpire has called "Play";

    (4)   fails to obey within a reasonable time the umpire's order to remove a player from the game;

    (5)   after warning by the umpire, willfully and persistently violates any rules of the game;

    (6)   employs tactics designed to delay or shorten the game.

**4.16** - If a game cannot be played because of the inability of either team to: 1. place nine players on the field before the game begins, and/or, 2. place at least one adult in the dugout as manager or acting manager, this shall not be grounds for automatic forfeiture, but shall be referred to the Board of Directors for a decision. **Note**: A game may not be started with less than nine (9) players on each team, nor without at least one adult manager or substitute manager.

**4.17** - If during a game either team is unable to place nine (9) players on the field due to injury or ejection, the opposing manager shall select a player to re-enter the lineup. A player ejected from the game is not eligible for re-entry. If no players are available for re-reentry, or if a team refuses to place nine (9) players on the field, this shall not be grounds for automatic forfeiture but shall be referred to the Board of Directors for a decision. **Note**: A game may not be continued with less than nine (9) players on each team.

**4.18** - Forfeited games shall be so recorded in the scorebook and the book signed by the umpire-in-chief. A written report stating the reason for the forfeiture shall be sent to the league president within 24 hours, but failure of the umpire to file this report shall not affect the forfeiture.

**4.19** - PROTESTING GAME

    (a)   Protest shall be considered only when based on the violation or interpretation of a playing rule, use of an ineligible pitcher or the use of an ineligible player. No protest shall be considered on a decision involving an umpire's judgment. Equipment which does not meet specifications must be removed from the game.

    (b)   The managers of contesting teams only shall have the right to protest a game (or in their absence, coaches). However, the manager or acting manager may not leave the dugout until receiving permission from an umpire.

(c) Protests shall be made as follows:
   (1) The protesting manager shall immediately, and before any succeed-ing play begins, notify the umpire that the game is being played under protest.
   (2) Following such notice the umpire shall consult with the other umpire(s). If the umpire is convinced that the decision is in conflict with the rules, the umpire shall reverse that decision. If, however, after consultation, the umpire is convinced that the decision is not in conflict with the rules, said umpire shall announce that the game is being played under protest. Failure of the umpire to make such announcement shall not affect the validity of the protest.

(d) Protest made due to use of Ineligible pitcher or ineligible player may be considered only if made to the umpire before the umpire(s) leave the field at the end of the game. Whenever it is found that an ineligible pitcher or ineligible player is being used, said pitcher shall be removed from the mound, or said player shall be removed from the game, and the game shall be continued under protest or not as the protesting manager decides.

(e) Any protest for any reason whatsoever must be submitted by the manager first to the umpire on the field of play and then in writing to the Local League president within 24 hours. The umpire-in-chief shall also submit a report immediately.

(f) A committee composed of the president, player agent, league's umpire-in-chief and one or more other officers or directors who are not managers or umpires shall hear and resolve any such protest as above, including playing rules. If the protest is allowed, resume the game from the exact point when the infraction occurred.

**NOTE**: (1) This rule does not pertain to charges of infractions of regu-lations such as field decorum or actions of the league personnel or spectators which must be considered and resolved by the Board of Directors.

**NOTE**: (2) All Little League officials are urged to take precautions to prevent protests. When a protest situation is imminent, the potential offenders should be notified immediately. **Example**: Should a manager, official scorer, league official or umpire discover that a pitcher is ineli-gible at the beginning of the game, or will become ineligible during the game or at the start of the next inning of play, the fact should be brought to the attention of the manager of the team involved. Such action should not be delayed until the infraction has occurred. However, failure of personnel to notify the manager of the infraction does not affect the validity of the protest.

(g) **Minor League**: A Local League may adopt a rule that protests must be resolved before the next pitch or play.

(h) There are no protests in Tee Ball.

### 5.00 - PUTTING THE BALL IN PLAY - LIVE BALL

**5.01** - At the time set for beginning the game the umpire-in-chief shall order the home team to take its defensive positions and the first batter of the visiting team to take a position in the batter's box. As soon as all players are in position the umpire-in-chief shall call "Play."

**5.02** - After the umpire calls "Play" the ball is alive and in play and remains alive and in play until, for legal cause, or at the umpire's call of "Time" suspending play, the ball becomes dead. While the ball is dead, no player may be put out, no bases may be run and no runs may be scored, except that runners may advance one or more bases as the result of acts which occurred while the ball was alive (such as, but not limited to an illegal pitch Junior/Senior/Big League - Balk, an overthrow, interference, or a home run or other fair hit out of the playing field.)

**5.03** - The pitcher shall deliver the pitch to the batter who may elect to strike the ball, or who may not offer at it, as such batter chooses.

**5.04** - The offensive team's objective is to have its batter become a runner, and its runners advance.

**5.05** - The defensive team's objective is to prevent offensive players from becoming runners, and to prevent their advance around the bases.

**5.06** - When a batter becomes a runner and touches all bases legally, one run shall be scored for the offensive team.

**5.07** - When three offensive players are legally put out, that team takes the field and the opposing team becomes the offensive team (side retired). (Minor League: The side is retired when three offensive players are legally put out, or when all players on the roster have batted one time in the half-inning, or when the offensive team scores five (5) runs. (**OPTION**: The local league board of directors may suspend the five-run rule in the last half-inning for either team.) Tee Ball: The side is retired when three offensive players are legally put out, or when all players on the roster have batted one time in the half-inning.)

**5.08** - If a thrown ball accidentally touches a base coach, or a pitched or thrown ball touches an umpire, the ball is alive and in play. However, if the base coach interferes with a thrown ball, the runner is out.

**5.09** - The ball becomes dead and runners advance one base, or return to their bases, without liability to be put out, when -

(a) a pitched ball touches a batter, or the batter's clothing, while in a legal batting position; runners, if forced, advance (see 6.08);

(b) the plate umpire interferes with the catcher's act of throwing (when the throw is in an attempt to retire a runner), runners return. If the catcher's throw gets the runner out, the out stands. No umpire interference;

(c) an illegal pitch (a balk in **Junior/Senior/Big League**) is committed (see Penalty 8.05);

(d) a ball is illegally batted either fair or foul; runners return;

(e) a foul ball not caught, runners return. The umpire shall not put the ball in play until all runners have retouched their bases;

(f) a fair ball touches a runner or an umpire on fair territory before it touches an infielder including the pitcher, or touches an umpire before it has passed an infielder other than the pitcher. Runner hit by a fair batted ball is out;

**NOTE**: If a fair ball goes through, or by an infielder and touches a runner immediately back of said infielder, or touches a runner after being deflected by an infielder, the ball is in play and the umpire shall not declare the runner out. In making such decision, the umpire must be convinced that the ball passed through, or by, the infielder and that no other infielder had the chance to make a play on the ball; runners advance, if forced;

(g) A pitched ball lodges in the catcher's or umpire's mask or paraphernalia; runners advance.

(h) (**Junior/Senior/Big League Baseball**) Any legal pitch touches a runner trying to score; runners advance.

**5.10** - The ball becomes dead when an umpire calls "Time." The umpire-in-chief shall call "Time" -

(a) when in said umpire's judgment, weather, darkness or similar conditions make immediate further play impossible;

(b) when light failure makes it difficult or impossible for the umpires to follow the play;
**NOTE**: A league may adopt its own regulations governing games interrupted by light failure.

(c) when an accident incapacitates a player or an umpire;
(1) If an accident to a runner is such as to prevent said runner from proceeding to an entitled base, as on a home run hit out of the playing field or an award of one or more bases, a substitute runner shall be permitted to complete the play.

(d) when a manager requests "Time" for a substitution, or for a conference with one of the players; (**NOTE**: Only one offensive time-out, for the purpose of a visit or conference, will be permitted each inning.)

(e) when the umpire wishes to examine the ball, to consult with either manager, or for any similar cause;

(f) when a fielder, after catching a fly ball, falls into a stand, or falls across ropes into a crowd when spectators are on the field, or any other dead-ball area. As pertains to runners, the provisions of 7.04(b) shall prevail. If a fielder after making a catch steps into a dead ball area, but does not fall, the ball is alive and in play and runners may advance at their own peril;

(g) when an umpire orders a player or any other person removed from the playing field;

(h) except in the cases stated in paragraphs (b) and (c) (1) of this rule, no umpire shall call "Time" while a play is in progress.

**5.11** - After the ball is dead, play shall be resumed when the pitcher takes a position on the pitcher's plate with a new ball or the same ball in said pitcher's possession and the plate umpire calls "Play." The plate umpire shall call "Play" as soon as the pitcher takes a position on the plate with possession of the ball.

<h2 style="text-align:center">6.00 - THE BATTER</h2>

**6.01** -

(a) Each player of the offensive team shall bat in the order that their name appears in the team's batting order.

(b) The first batter in each inning after the first inning shall be the player whose name follows that of the last player who legally completed a time at bat in the preceding inning
**NOTE**: In the event that while a batter is in the batter's box, the third out of an inning is made on a base runner, the batter then at bat shall be the first batter of the next inning and the count of balls and strikes

shall start over.

**6.02** -

(a) The batter shall take his/her position in the batter's box promptly when it is said batter's time at bat.

(b) The batter shall not leave that position in the batter's box after the pitcher comes to Set Position, or starts a windup.

**PENALTY**: If the pitcher pitches, the umpire shall call "Ball" or "Strike" as the case may be.

(c) If the batter refuses to take his/her position in the batter's box during a time at bat, the umpire shall call a strike on the batter without the need for a pitch to be delivered. The ball is dead, and no runners may advance. After the penalty, the batter may take a proper position, and the regular ball and strike count shall continue, but if the batter does not take the proper position before three strikes are called, that batter shall be declared out.

**6.03** - The batter's legal position shall be with both feet within the batter's box.

**APPROVED RULING**: The lines defining the box are within the batter's box.

**6.04** - A batter has legally completed a time at bat when he/she is put out or becomes a runner.

**6.05** - A batter is out when -

(a) a fair or foul fly ball (other than a foul tip) is legally caught by a fielder;

(b) a third strike is caught or not caught by the catcher (**Junior/Senior/ Big League**: (1) a third strike is legally caught by the catcher; (2) a third strike is not caught by the catcher when first base is occupied before two are out);

(c) bunting foul on a third strike;

(d) an Infield Fly is declared;

(e) that batter attempts to hit a third strike and is touched by the ball;

(f) a fair ball touches said batter before touching a fielder;

(g) after hitting or bunting a fair ball, the bat hits the ball a second time in fair territory. The ball is dead and no runner may advance. If the batter-runner drops the bat and the ball rolls against the bat in fair territory and, in the umpire's judgment there was no intention to interfere with the course of the ball, the ball is alive and in play;

(h) after hitting or bunting a foul ball, the batter-runner intentionally deflects the course of the ball in any manner while running to first base. The ball is dead and no runners may advance;

(i) after hitting a fair ball, the batter-runner or first base is tagged before said batter-runner touches first base; or **Junior/Senior/Big League**, after a third strike as defined in Rule 6.09(b), the batter-runner or first base is tagged before said batter-runner touches first base;

(j) in running the last half of the distance from home base to first base, while the ball is being fielded to first base, the batter-runner runs outside (to the right of) the three-foot line, or inside (to the left of) the foul line, and in the umpire's judgment in so doing interferes with the fielder taking the throw at first base; except that the batter-runner may run outside (to the right of) the three-foot line or inside (to the left of) the foul line to avoid a fielder attempting to field a batted ball;

(k)  an infielder intentionally drops a fair fly ball or line drive, with first, first and second, first and third, or first, second and third bases occupied before two are out. The ball is dead and runner or runners shall return to their original base or bases;

APPROVED RULING: In this situation, the batter is not out if the infielder permits the ball to drop untouched to the ground, except when the Infield Fly rule applies.

(l)  a preceding runner shall, in the umpire's judgment, intentionally interfere with a fielder who is attempting to catch a thrown ball or to throw a ball in an attempt to complete a play.

(m)  **Junior/Senior/Big League**: with two out, a runner on third base, and two strikes on the batter, the runner attempts to steal home base on a legal pitch and the ball touches the runner in the batter's strike zone. The umpire shall call "Strike Three," the batter is out and the run shall not count; before two are out, the umpire shall call "Strike Three," the ball is dead, and the run counts.

**6.06** - A batter is out for illegal action when -

(a)  hitting the ball with one or both feet on the ground entirely outside the batter's box.

(b)  stepping from one batter's box to the other while the pitcher is in position ready to pitch;

(c)  interfering with the catcher's fielding or throwing by stepping out of the batter's box or making any other movement that hinders the catcher's play at home base.

EXCEPTION: Batter is not out if any runner attempting to advance is put out, or if runner trying to score is called out for batter's interference.

## 6.07 - BATTING OUT OF TURN

(a)  A batter shall be called out, on appeal, when failing to bat in his/her proper turn, and another batter completes a time at bat in place of the proper batter. (1) The proper batter may take a position in the batter's box at any time before the improper batter becomes a runner or is put out, and any balls and strikes shall be counted in the proper batter's time at bat.

(b)  When an improper batter becomes a runner or is put out, and the defensive team appeals to the umpire before the first pitch to the next batter of either team, or before any play or attempted play, the umpire shall (1) declare the proper batter out; and (2) nullify any advance or score made because of a ball batted by the improper batter or because of the improper batter's advance to first base on a hit, an error, a base on balls, a hit batter or otherwise.

NOTE: If a runner advances, while the improper batter is at bat, on a stolen base, illegal pitch, **Junior/Senior/Big League** balk, wild pitch or passed ball, such advance is legal.

(c)  When an improper batter becomes a runner or is put out, and a pitch is made to the next batter of either team before an appeal is made, the improper batter thereby becomes the proper batter, and the results of such time at bat become legal.

(d)  (1) When the proper batter is called out for failing to bat in turn, the next batter shall be the batter whose name follows that of the proper batter thus called out; (2) When an improper batter becomes a proper batter because no appeal is made before the next pitch, the next batter shall be the batter whose name follows that of such legalized improper batter. The instant an improper batter's actions are legalized, the batting order picks up with the name following that of the legalized improper batter.

**APPROVED RULINGS**

To illustrate various situations arising from batting out of turn, assume a first-inning batting order as follows:

Abel - Baker - Charles - Daniel - Edward - Frank - George - Henry - Irwin.

PLAY (1). Baker bats. With the count 2 balls and 1 strike, (a) the offensive team discovers the error or (b) the defensive team appeals.

**RULING**: In either case, Abel replaces Baker, with the count 2 balls and 1 strike.

PLAY (2). Baker bats and doubles. The defensive team appeals (a) immediately or (b) after a pitch to Charles.

**RULING**: (a) Abel is called out and Baker is the proper batter; (b) Baker stays on second and Charles is the proper batter.

PLAY (3). Abel walks. Baker walks. Charles forces Baker. Edward bats in Daniel's turn. While Edward is at bat, Abel scores and Charles goes to second on a wild pitch. Edward grounds out, sending Charles to third. The defensive team appeals (a) immediately or (b) after a pitch to Daniel.

**RULING**: (a) Abel's run counts and Charles is entitled to second base since these advances were not made because of the improper batter batting a ball or advancing to first base. Charles must return to second base because the advance to third resulted from the improper batter batting a ball. Daniel is called out and Edward is the proper batter; (b) Abel's run counts and Charles stays on third. The proper batter is Frank.

PLAY (4). With the bases full and two out, Henry bats in Frank's turn, and triples, scoring three runs. The defensive team appeals (a) immediately or (b) after a pitch to George.

**RULING**: (a) Frank is called out and no runs score. George is the proper batter to lead off the second inning; (b) Henry stays on third and three runs score. Irwin is the proper batter.

PLAY (5). After Play (4) (b) above, George continues to bat. (a) Henry is picked off third base for the third out, or (b) George flies out, and no appeal is made. Who is the proper leadoff batter in the second inning?

**RULING**: (a) Irwin became the proper batter as soon as the first pitch to George legalized Henry's triple; (b) Henry. When no appeal was made, the first pitch to the leadoff batter of the opposing team legalized George's time at bat.

PLAY (6). Daniel walks and Abel comes to bat. Daniel was an improper batter and if an appeal is made before the first pitch to Abel, Abel is out, Daniel is removed from base, and Baker is proper batter. There is no appeal and a pitch is made to Abel. Daniel's walk is now legalized, and Edward thereby becomes the proper batter. Edward can replace Abel at any time before Abel is put out, or becomes a runner. Edward does not do so. Abel flies out, and Baker comes to bat. Abel was an improper batter, and if an appeal is made before the first pitch to Baker, Edward is out, and the proper batter is Frank. There is no appeal, and a pitch is made to Baker. Abel's out is now legalized, and the proper batter is Baker. Baker walks. Charles is the proper batter. Charles flies out. Now Daniel is the proper batter, but Daniel is on second base. Who is the proper batter?

**RULING**: The proper batter is Edward. When the proper batter is on base, that batter is passed over, and the following batter becomes the proper batter.

(**NOTE**: The umpire and scorekeeper shall not direct the attention of any person to the presence in the batter's box of an improper batter. This rule is designed to require constant vigilance by the players and managers of both teams. There are two fundamentals to keep in mind: 1. When a player bats out of turn, the proper batter is the player called out. 2. If an improper batter bats and reaches base or is out and no appeal is made before a pitch to the next batter, or before any play or attempted play, that improper batter is considered to have batted in proper turn and establishes the order that is to follow.)

**Tee Ball**: The scorekeeper shall inform the manager that a player has batted out of order. There shall be no penalty and that player shall not have another turn at bat, but shall resume the normal position next time up.

**6.08** - The batter becomes a runner and is entitled to first base without liability to be put out (provided said runner advances to and touches first base) when -

(a)  four "balls" have been called by the umpire; base runners may advance;

(b)  the batter is touched by a pitched ball which the batter is not attempting to hit unless (1) The ball is in the strike zone when it touches the batter, or (2) the batter makes no attempt to avoid being touched by the ball;

  **NOTE**: If the ball is in the strike zone when it touches the batter, it shall be called a strike, whether or not the batter tries to avoid the ball. If the ball is outside the strike zone when it touches the batter, it shall be called a ball if that batter makes no attempt to avoid being touched.

  **APPROVED RULING**: When the batter is touched by a pitched ball which does not entitle that batter to first base, the ball is dead and no runner may advance.

(c)  the catcher or any fielder interferes with the batter. If a play follows the interference, the manager of the offense may advise the plate umpire of a decision to decline the interference penalty and accept the play. Such election shall be made immediately at the end of the play. However, if the batter reaches first base on a hit, an error, a base on balls, a hit batter, or otherwise, and all other runners advance at least one base, the play proceeds without reference to the interference;

(d)  a fair ball touches an umpire or a runner in fair territory before touching a fielder.

  **NOTE**: If a fair ball touches an umpire after having passed a fielder other than the pitcher, or having touched a fielder, including the pitcher, the ball is in play.

**6.09** - The batter becomes a runner when-

(a)  a fair ball is hit;

(b)  **Junior/Senior/Big League** only: the third strike called by the umpire is not caught, providing (1) first base is unoccupied or (2) first base is occupied with two out (**NOTE**: A batter forfeits his/her opportunity to advance to first base when he/she enters the dugout or other dead ball area);

(c) a fair ball, after having passed a fielder other than the pitcher, or after having been touched by a fielder, including the pitcher, shall touch an umpire or runner in fair territory;

(d) a fair fly ball passes over a fence or into the stands at a distance from home base of 165 feet (**Junior/Senior/Big League**: 250 feet) or more. Such hit entitles the batter to a home run when all bases have been legally touched. A fair fly ball that passes out of the playing field at a point less than 165 feet (**Junior/Senior/Big League**: 250 feet) from home base shall entitle the batter to advance to second base only;

(e) a fair ball, after touching the ground, bounds into the stands, or passes through, over or under a fence, or through or under a scoreboard, or through or under shrubbery, or vines on the fence, in which case the batter and runners shall be entitled to advance two bases;

(f) any fair ball which, either before or after touching the ground, passes through or under a fence, or through or under a scoreboard, or through any opening in the fence or scoreboard, or through or under shrubbery or vines on the fence, or which sticks in a fence or scoreboard, in which case the batter and the runners shall be entitled to two bases;

(g) any bounding fair ball is deflected by the fielder into the stands, or over or under a fence on fair or foul territory, in which case the batter and all runners shall be entitled to advance two bases;

(h) any fair fly ball is deflected by the fielder into the stands, or over the fence into foul territory, in which case the batter shall be entitled to advance to second base; but if deflected into the stands or over the fence in fair territory, the batter shall be entitled to a home run. However, should such a fair fly be deflected at a point less than 165 feet (**Junior/Senior/Big League**: 250 feet) from home plate, the batter shall be entitled to two bases only.

### 7.00 - THE RUNNER

**7.01** - A runner acquires the right to an unoccupied base when that runner touches it before being put out. The runner is then entitled to it until put out or forced to vacate it for another runner legally entitled to that base. If a runner legally acquires title to a base, and the pitcher assumes his/her position on the pitcher's plate, the runner may not return to a previously occupied base.

**7.02** - In advancing, a runner shall touch first, second, third and home base in order.

If forced to return, the runner shall retouch all bases in reverse order, unless the ball is dead under any provision of Rule 5.09. In such cases, the runner may go directly to the original base.

**7.03** - Two runners may not occupy a base, but if, while the ball is alive, two runners are touching the base, the following runner shall be out when tagged. The preceding runner is entitled to the base.

**7.04** - Each runner, other than the batter, may, without liability to be put out, advance one base when -

(a) the batter's advance without liability to be put out forces the runner to vacate a base, or when the batter hits a fair ball that touches another runner or the umpire before such ball has been touched by, or has passed a fielder, if the runner is forced to advance, or in **Junior/Senior/ Big League Baseball**, there is a balk;

(b) a fielder, after catching a fly ball, falls into a stand, or falls across ropes into a crowd when spectators are on the field or falls into any other dead-ball areas;

(c) **Junior/Senior/Big League**: while the runner is attempting to steal a base, the batter is interfered with by the catcher or any other fielder.

**NOTE:** When a runner is entitled to a base without liability to be put out, while the ball is in play, or under any rule in which the ball is in play after the runner reaches an entitled base, and the runner fails to touch the base to which that runner is entitled before attempting to advance to the next base, the runner shall forfeit the exemption from liability to be put out and may be put out by tagging the base or by tagging the runner before that runner returns to the missed base.

**7.05** - Each runner including the batter-runner may, without liability to be put out, advance -

(a) to home base scoring a run, if a fair ball goes out of the playing field in flight and the runner touches all bases legally; or if a fair ball which, in the umpire's judgment, would have gone out of the playing field in flight (165 feet from home plate; **Junior/Senior/Big League** 250 feet), is deflected by the act of a fielder in throwing a glove, cap, or any article of apparel;

(b) three bases, if a fielder deliberately touches a fair ball with a cap, mask, or any part of that fielder's uniform detached from its proper place on the person of said fielder. The ball is in play and the batter may advance to home plate at the batter's peril;

(c) three bases, if a fielder deliberately throws a glove and touches a fair ball. The ball is in play and the batter may advance to home plate at that batter's own peril;

(d) two bases, if a fielder deliberately touches a thrown ball with a cap, mask or any part of the uniform detached from its proper place on the person of said fielder. The ball is in play;

(e) two bases, if a fielder deliberately throws a glove at and touches a thrown ball. The ball is in play;

(f) two bases, if a fair ball bounces or is deflected into the stands outside the first or third base foul line; or if it goes through or under a field fence, or through or under a scoreboard, or through or under shrubbery or vines on the fence; or if it sticks in such fence, scoreboard, shrubbery or vines;

(g) two bases when, with no spectators on the playing field, a thrown ball goes into the stands, or into a bench (whether or not the ball rebounds into the field), or over or under or through a field fence, or on a slanting part of the screen above the backstop, or remains in the meshes of the wire screen protecting spectators. The ball is dead. When such a wild throw is the first play by an infielder, the umpire, in awarding such bases, shall be governed by the position of the runners at the time the ball was pitched; in all other cases the umpire shall be governed by the position of the runners at the time the wild throw was made;

**APPROVED RULING**: If all runners, including the batter-runner have advanced at least one base when an infielder makes a wild throw on the first play after the pitch, the award shall be governed by the position of the runners when the wild throw was made.

(h) one base, if a ball, pitched to the batter, or thrown by the pitcher from the position on the pitcher's plate to a base to catch a runner goes into a stand or a bench, or over or through a field fence or backstop. The ball is dead;

(i) one base, if the batter becomes a runner on a ball four when the pitch passes the catcher and lodges in the umpire's mask or paraphernalia. **Junior/Senior/Big League**: one base, if the batter becomes a runner on a ball four or strike three when the pitch passes the catcher and lodges in the umpire's mask or paraphernalia.

**NOTE (1)**: If the batter becomes a runner on a wild pitch which entitles the runners to advance one base, the batter-runner shall be entitled to first base only but can advance beyond first base at their own risk if the ball stays in play.

**NOTE (2)**: In Tee Ball, the runner or runners will be permitted to advance at their own risk on an overthrow that remains in play, but not more than one base.

(j) one base, if a fielder deliberately touches a pitched ball with his/her cap, mask or any part of his/her uniform detached from its proper place on his/her person. The ball is in play, and the award is made based on the position of the runner at the time the ball was touched.

**7.06** - When the obstruction occurs, the umpire shall call or signal "Obstruction."

(a) If a play is being made on the obstructed runner, or if the batter-runner is obstructed before touching first base, the ball is dead and all runners shall advance without liability to be put out, to the bases they would have reached, in the umpire's judgment, if there had been no obstruction. The obstructed runner shall be awarded at least one base beyond the base last legally touched by such runner, before the obstruction. Any preceding runners forced to advance by the award of bases as the penalty for obstruction shall advance without liability to be put out;

(b) If no play is being made on the obstructed runner, the play shall proceed until no further action is possible. The umpire shall then call "Time" and impose such penalties, if any, as in that umpire's judgment will nullify the act of obstruction. (**NOTE 1**: When the ball is not dead on obstruction and an obstructed runner advances beyond the base which, in the umpire's judgment, the runner would have been awarded because of being obstructed, the runner does so at his/her own risk and may be tagged out. This is a judgment call. **NOTE 2**: If the defensive player blocks the base (plate) or base line clearly without possession of the ball, obstruction shall be called. The runner is safe and a delayed dead ball shall be called.

**7.07** - **Junior/Senior/Big League Baseball**: If, with a runner on third base and trying to score by means of a squeeze play or steal, the catcher or any other fielder steps on or in front of home base without possession of the ball, or touches the batter or the bat, the pitcher shall be charged with a balk, the batter shall be awarded first base on the interference and the ball is dead.

**7.08** - Any runner is out when -

(a) (1) running more than three feet away from his/her baseline to avoid being tagged, unless such action is to avoid interference with a fielder fielding a batted ball. A runner's baseline is established when the tag attempt occurs, and is a straight line from the runner to the base to which he/she is attempting to reach; or (2) after touching first base the runner leaves the baseline, obviously abandoning all effort to touch the next base; or (3) the runner does not slide or attempt to get around a fielder who has the ball and is waiting to make the tag; (4) **Tee Ball, Little League Majors and Minors only**: the runner slides head first while advancing.

**APPROVED RULING (Junior/Senior/Big League Baseball)**: When a batter becomes a runner on a third strike not caught and starts for the bench or his/her position, that batter may advance to first base at any time before entering the bench. To put the batter out, the defense must tag the batter or first base before the batter touches first base.

(b) intentionally interferes with a thrown ball; or hinders a fielder attempting to make a play on a batted ball (**NOTE**: A runner who is adjudged to have hindered a fielder who is attempting to make a play on a batted ball is out whether it was intentional or not);

(c) that runner is tagged, when the ball is alive, while off a base;

**EXCEPTION**: A batter-runner cannot be tagged out after overrunning or oversliding first base if said batter-runner returns immediately to the base.

**APPROVED RULING**: (1) If the impact of a runner breaks a base loose from its position, no play can be made on that runner at that base if the runner had reached the base safely.

**APPROVED RULING**: (2) If a base is dislodged from its position during a play, any following runner on the same play shall be considered as touching or occupying the base if, in the umpire's judgment, that runner touches or occupies the dislodged bag, or the point marked by the original location of the dislodged bag.

(d) failing to retouch the base after a fair or foul fly ball is legally caught before that runner or the base is tagged by a fielder. The runner shall not be called out for failure to retouch the base after the first following pitch, or any play or attempted play. This is an appeal play.

**NOTE**: Base runners can legally retouch their base once a fair ball is touched in flight and advance at their own risk if a fair or foul ball is caught.

(e) failing to reach the next base before a fielder tags said runner or the base after that runner has been forced to advance by reason of the batter becoming a runner. However, if a following runner is put out on a force play, the force is removed and the runner must be tagged to be put out. The force is removed as soon as the runner touches the base to which that runner is forced to advance, and if oversliding or overrunning the base, the runner must be tagged to be put out. However, if the forced runner, after touching the next base, retreats for any reason towards the base last occupied, the force play is reinstated and the runner can again be put out if the defense tags the base to which the runner is forced;

(f)    touched by a fair ball in fair territory before the ball has touched or passed an infielder. The ball is dead and no runner may score, no runners may advance, except runners forced to advance;

**EXCEPTION**: If a runner is touching a base when touched by an Infield Fly, that runner is not out, although the batter is out.

**NOTE 1**: If a runner is touched by an Infield Fly when not touching a base, both runner and batter are out.

**NOTE 2**: If two runners are touched by the same fair ball, only the first one is out because the ball is instantly dead.

(g)    attempting to score on a play in which the batter interferes with the play at home base before two are out. With two out, the interference puts the batter out and no score counts;

(h)    passes a preceding runner before such runner is out;

(i)    after acquiring legal possession of a base, the runner runs the bases in reverse order for the purpose of confusing the defense or making a travesty of the game. The umpire shall immediately call "Time" and declare the runner out;

(j)    failing to return at once to first base after overrunning or oversliding that base. If attempting to run to second the runner is out when tagged. If after overrunning or oversliding first base, the runner starts toward the dugout, or toward a position, and fails to return to first base at once, that runner is out on appeal, when said runner or the base is tagged;

(k)    in running or sliding for home base, the runner fails to touch home base and makes no attempt to return to the base, when a fielder holds the ball in hand, while touching home base, and appeals to the umpire for the decision. (**NOTE**: This rule applies only where the runner is on the way to the bench and a fielder would be required to chase the runner to tag him/her. It does not apply to the ordinary play where the runner misses the plate and then immediately makes an effort to touch the plate before being tagged. In that case, the runner must be tagged.)

**7.09** - It is interference by a batter or runner when -

(a)    the batter hinders the catcher in an attempt to field the ball;

(b)    the batter intentionally deflects the course of a foul ball in any manner;

(c)    before two are out and a runner on third base, the batter hinders a fielder in making a play at home base; the runner is out;

(d)    any member or members of the offensive team stand or gather around any base to which a runner is advancing, to confuse, hinder or add to the difficulty of the fielders. Such runner shall be declared out for the interference of teammate or teammates;

(e)    any batter or runner who has just been put out hinders or impedes any following play being made on a runner. Such runner shall be declared out for the interference of a teammate;

(f)    if, in the judgment of the umpire, a base runner willfully and deliberately interferes with a batted ball or a fielder in the act of fielding a batted ball with the obvious intent to break up a double play, the ball is dead.

The umpire shall call the runner out for interference and also call out the batter-runner because of the action of the runner. In no event may bases be run or runs scored because of such action by a runner;

(g)  if, in the judgment of the umpire, a batter-runner willfully and deliberately interferes with a batted ball or a fielder in the act of fielding a batted ball, with the obvious intent to break up a double play, the ball is dead. The umpire shall call the batter-runner out for interference and shall also call out the runner who advanced closest to the home plate regardless where the double play might have been possible. In no event shall bases be run because of such interference;

(h)  in the judgment of the umpire, the base coach at third base, or first base, by touching or holding the runner, physically assists that runner in returning to or leaving third base or first base;

(i)  with a runner on third base, the base coach leaves the box and acts in any manner to draw a throw by a fielder;

(j)  the runner fails to avoid a fielder who is attempting to field a batted ball, or intentionally interferes with a thrown ball, provided that if two or more fielders attempt to field a batted ball and the runner comes in contact with one or more of them, the umpire shall determine which fielder is entitled to the benefit of this rule, and shall not declare the runner out for coming in contact with a fielder other than the one the umpire determines to be entitled to field such a ball;

(k)  a fair ball touches the batter or runner in fair territory before touching a fielder. If a fair ball goes through or by an infielder and touches a runner immediately back of said infielder or touches the runner after having been deflected by a fielder, the umpire shall not declare the runner out for being touched by a batted ball. In making such decision, the umpire must be convinced that the ball passed through or by the infielder and that no other infielder had the chance to make a play on the ball. If in the judgment of the umpire, the runner deliberately and intentionally kicks such a batted ball on which the infielder had missed a play, then the runner shall be called out for interference.

**PENALTY FOR INTERFERENCE**: The runner is out and the ball is dead.

**7.10** - Any runner shall be called out on appeal if-

(a)  after a fly ball is caught the runner fails to retouch the base before said runner or the base is tagged (**NOTE**: "Retouch" in this rule means to tag up and start from a contact with the base after the ball is caught. A runner is not permitted to take a flying start from a position in back of, and not touching, the base);

(b)  with the ball in play, while advancing or returning to a base, the runner fails to touch each base in order before said runner, or a missed base, is tagged;

**APPROVED RULING**: (1) No runner may return to touch a missed base after a following runner has scored. (2) When the ball is dead no runner may return to touch a missed base or one abandoned after said runner has advanced to and touched a base beyond the missed base.

**Play A** - Batter hits the ball out of the park, or hits a ground rule double, and misses first base (ball is dead). The runner may return to first base to correct the mistake before touching second. But if the runner touches second, he/she may not return to first and if the defensive team appeals, the runner is declared out at first. (**Appeal play**.)

**Play B** - Batter hits a ground ball to shortstop, who throws wild into the stands (ball is dead). Batter-runner misses first base but is awarded second base on the overthrow. Even though the umpire has awarded the runner second base on the overthrow, the runner must touch first base before proceeding to second base. (**Appeal play**.)

(c) the runner overruns or overslides first base and fails to return to the base immediately, and said runner or the base is tagged;

(d) the runner fails to touch home base and makes no attempt to return to that base, and home base is tagged. **NOTE**: A runner forfeits his/her opportunity to return to home base when he/she enters the dugout or other dead ball area.

Any appeal under this rule must be made before the next pitch, or any play or attempted play. No appeal can be made if the ball is dead. If the violation occurs during a play which ends a half-inning, the appeal must be made before all the defensive players have left fair territory on their way to the bench or dugout. **EXCEPTION:** If an otherwise proper appeal is being made by a player who has to go into foul territory to retrieve the ball in order to make an appeal or if the appeal is being made by the catcher (who may never have been in fair territory at all), the appeal will be adjudged to have been properly executed.

An appeal is not to be interpreted as a play or an attempted play.

Successive appeals may not be made on a runner at the same base. If the defensive team on its first appeal errs, a request for a second appeal on the same runner at the same base shall not be allowed by the umpire. (Intended meaning of the word "err" is that the defensive team in making an appeal threw the ball out of play. For example, if the pitcher threw to first base to appeal and threw the ball into the stands, no second appeal would be allowed.)

**NOTE**: (1) Appeal plays may require an umpire to recognize an apparent "fourth out." If the third out is made during a play in which an appeal play is sustained on another runner, the appeal play decision takes precedence in determining the out. If there is more than one appeal during a play that ends a half-inning, the defense may elect to take the out that gives it the advantage. For the purposes of this rule, the defensive team has "left the field" when all players have left fair territory on their way to the bench or dugout.

**NOTE**: (2) If a pitcher makes an illegal pitch (a balk in **Junior/Senior/Big League baseball**) when making an appeal, such act shall be a play. An appeal should be clearly intended as an appeal, either by a verbal request by the player or an act that unmistakably indicates an appeal to the umpire. A player, inadvertently stepping on the base with a ball in hand, would not constitute an appeal. The ball must be alive and in play.

**7.11** - The players, coaches or any member of an offensive team shall vacate any space (including both dugouts) needed by a fielder who is attempting to field a batted or thrown ball.

**PENALTY**: Interference shall be called and the batter or runner on whom the play is being made shall be declared out.

**7.12** - Unless two are out, the status of a following runner is not affected by a preceding runner's failure to touch or retouch a base. If, upon appeal, the preceding runner is the third out, no runners following the preceding runner shall score. If such third out is the result of a force play, neither preceding nor following runners shall score.

**7.13** - **Little League (Majors) and Minor League:** When a pitcher is in contact with the pitcher's plate and in possession of the ball and the catcher is in the catcher's box ready to receive delivery of the ball, base runners shall not leave their bases until the ball has been delivered and has reached the batter. **NOTE**: In Tee Ball, base runners must stay in contact with the base until the ball is hit. When players have advanced as far as possible without being put out or having been retired, the umpire shall call "time" and place the ball on the tee.

The violation by one base runner shall affect all other base runners -

    (a)   when a base runner leaves the base before the pitched ball has reached the batter and the batter does not hit the ball, the runner is permitted to continue. If a play is made on the runner and the runner is out, the out stands. If said runner reaches safely the base to which the runner is advancing, that runner must be returned to the base occupied before the pitch was made, and no out results;

    (b)   when a base runner leaves the base before the pitched ball has reached the batter and the batter hits the ball, the base runner or runners are permitted to continue. If a play is made and the runner or runners are put out, the out or outs will stand. If not put out, the runner or runners must return to the original base or bases or to the unoccupied base nearest the one that was left;

        In no event shall the batter advance beyond first base on a single or error, second base on a double or third base on a triple. The umpire-in-chief shall determine the base value of the hit ball.

    (c)   when any base runner leaves the base before the pitched ball has reached the batter and the batter bunts or hits a ball within the infield, no run shall be allowed to score. If three runners were on the bases and the batter reaches first base safely, each runner shall advance to the base beyond the one they occupied at the start of the play except the runner who occupied third base, that runner shall be removed from the base without a run being scored.

        **NOTE**: See exceptions following this rule.

        **EXCEPTION**: If at the conclusion of the play there is an open base, paragraphs (a) and (b) will apply.

**EXAMPLES**:

1. Runner on first leaves too soon, batter reaches first safely, runner goes to second.
2. Runner on second leaves too soon, batter reaches first safely, runner returns to second.
3. Runner on third leaves too soon, batter reaches first safely, runner returns to third.

4. Runner on first leaves too soon, batter hits clean double, runner goes to third only.
5. Runner on second leaves too soon, batter hits clean double, runner goes to third only.
6. Runner on third leaves too soon, batter hits clean double, runner returns to third.
7. All runners on base will be allowed to score when the batter hits a clean triple or home run, regardless of whether any runner left too soon.
8. Runners on first and second, either leaves too soon, batter reaches first safely, runners go to second and third.
9. Runners on first and second, either leaves too soon, batter hits clean double, runner on first goes to third, runner on second scores.
10. Runners on first and third, either leaves too soon, batter reaches first safely, runner on first goes to second, runner on third remains there.
11. Runners on first and third, either leaves too soon, batter hits a clean double, runner on first goes to third, runner on third scores.
12. Runners on second and third, either leaves too soon, batter reaches first safely, neither runner can advance.
13. Runners on second and third, either leaves too soon, batter hits a clean double, runner on third scores, runner on second goes to third.
14. Runners on first, second and third, any runner leaves too soon, batter hits clean double, runners on second, third score, runner on first goes to third.
15. Bases full, any runner leaves too soon, batter reaches first safely on any ball bunted or hit within the infield, all runners advance one base except runner advancing from third. Runner advancing from third is removed, no run is scored and no out charged. If on the play, a putout at any base results in an open base, runner who occupied third base returns to third base.
16. Bases full, any runner leaves too soon, batter received a base on balls or is hit by a pitch, each runner will advance one base and a run will score.

**NOTE (1)**: When an umpire detects a base runner leaving the base too soon, that umpire shall drop a signal flag or handkerchief immediately to indicate the violation.

**NOTE (2)**: For purpose of these examples, it is assumed that the batter-runner remains at the base last acquired safely.

**NOTE (3)**: In Tee Ball, base runners must stay in contact with the base until the ball is hit. When players have advanced as far as possible without being put out or having been retired the umpire shall call "time" and place the ball on the tee.

**7.14** - Once each inning a team may utilize a player who is not in the batting order as a special pinch-runner for any offensive player. A player may only be removed for a special pinch runner one time during a game. The player for whom the pinch-runner runs is not subject to removal from the lineup. If the pinch runner remains in the game as a substitute defensive or offensive player, the player may not be used again as a pinch runner while in the batting order. However, if removed for another substitute that player or any player not in the line up, is again eligible to be used as a pinch runner. **NOTE: Does not apply if the local league adopts the continuous batting order. See Rule 4.04.**

**7.15** - Procedures for Use of a Double First Base: The double base may be used for first base only. The base must be rectangular, with two sides not less than 14 inches and not more than 15 inches, and the other two side not less than 29 inches and not more than 30 inches. The longer sides shall face toward home plate and the right field corner. The outer edges shall not be more than two and one-fourth (2 ¼) inches thick, filled with soft material, and covered with canvas or rubber. Half the base shall be white (entirely over fair territory) and half shall be orange or green (entirely over foul territory). When using the double first base, the following rules must be observed:

(a) A batted ball that hits the white section of the double base shall be declared fair. A batted ball that hits the colored (orange or green) section without first touching or bounding over the white section shall be declared foul.

(b) Whenever a play is being made on the batter-runner, the defense must use the white section of the double first base. **NOTE 1:** A play is being made on the batter-runner when he/she is attempting to reach first base while the defense is attempting to retire him/her at that base. **NOTE 2: If there is a play on the batter-runner, and the batter-runner touches only the white portion and the defense appeals prior to the batter-runner returning to first base, it is treated the same as missing the base. Penalty: Batter-runner is out.**

(c) Whenever a play is being made on the batter-runner, the batter-runner must use the colored (orange or green) section on his/her first attempt to tag first base. **NOTE**: On extra-base hits or other balls hit to the outfield when there is no chance for a play to be made at the double first base, the batter-runner may touch either the white or colored (orange or green) section of the base. Should, however, the batter-runner reach and go beyond first base, he/she may only return to the white section of the base. **Penalty: If there is a play on the batter-runner, and the batter-runner touches only the white portion and the defense appeals prior to the batter-runner returning to first base, it is treated the same as missing the base. If properly appealed, the batter-runner is out.**

(d) When tagging up on a fly ball, the white section of the base must be used by the runner. One foot is permitted to extend behind or on the base into foul territory, as long as the front foot is touching the white section of the base. **Penalty: If properly appealed, runner is out.**

(e) When leaving base on a pitched ball in Little League Baseball (Majors and below), the runner must maintain contact with the white section of the base until the ball has reached the batter. Runners may extend a foot behind the white portion of the base, but must maintain contact with the white section until the ball has reached the batter. **Penalty: See Rule 7.13.**

(f) On an attempted pick-off play, the runner must return to the white section of the base only. This includes a throw from the pitcher, catcher, or any other player, in an attempt to retire the runner at the double first base.

(g) In **Junior, Senior and Big League** divisions, when the batter becomes a runner on a third strike not caught by the catcher, the batter-runner and the defensive player may use either the colored (orange or green) or the white section.

(h) Use of the double first base does not change any other rule concerning interference or obstruction at first base. (An errant throw into the three-foot running lane could still result in an obstruction call. Also, the batter-runner must still avoid interference with the fielder attempting to field a batted ball.)

## 8.00 - THE PITCHER

**8.01** - Legal pitching delivery. There are two legal pitching positions, the Windup Position and the Set Position, and either position may be used at any time.

Pitchers shall take signs from the catcher while standing on the pitcher's plate. Pitchers may disengage the pitcher's plate after taking their signs but may not step quickly onto the pitcher's plate and pitch. This may be judged a quick pitch by the umpire. When the pitcher disengages the pitcher's plate, he/she must drop the hands to the sides.

(a) The Windup Position. The pitcher shall stand facing the batter, the pivot foot in contact with the pitcher's plate, and the other foot free. From this position any natural movement associated with the delivery of the ball to the batter commits the pitcher to pitch without interruption or alteration. The pitcher shall not raise either foot from the ground, except that in the actual delivery of the ball to the batter, said pitcher may take one step backward, and one step forward with the free foot. From this position the pitcher may:

(1) deliver the ball to the batter, or

(2) step and throw to a base in an attempt to pick off a runner, or

(3) disengage the pitcher's plate. In disengaging the pitcher's plate, the pitcher must step off with the pivot foot and not the free foot first. The pitcher may not go into a set or stretch position. If the pitcher does, it is an illegal pitch (**a balk in Junior/Senior/Big League Baseball**).

**NOTE**: When a pitcher holds the ball with both hands in front of the body, with the pivot foot in contact with the pitcher's plate, and the other foot free, that pitcher will be considered in a Windup Position.

(b) The Set Position. Set Position shall be indicated by the pitcher when that pitcher stands facing the batter with the pivot foot in contact with and the other foot in front of the pitcher's plate, holding the ball in both hands in front of the body and coming to a complete stop. From such Set Position the pitcher may deliver the ball to the batter, throw to a base or step backward off the pitcher's plate with the pivot foot. Before assuming the Set Position, the pitcher may elect to make any natural preliminary motion such as that known as "the stretch." But if the pitcher so elects, that pitcher shall come to the Set Position before delivering the ball to that batter.

**NOTE**: In Little League (Majors) and below the pitcher need not come to a complete stop. **Junior/Senior/Big League**: the pitcher must come to a complete and discernible stop.

(c) At any time during the pitcher's preliminary movements and until the natural pitching motion commits that pitcher to the pitch, said pitcher may throw to any base provided the pitcher steps directly toward such base before making the throw. The pitcher shall step "ahead of the throw." A snap throw followed by the step toward the base is an illegal pitch **(A balk in Junior/Senior/Big League baseball)**. (See Penalty for illegal pitch/balk under Rule 8.05.)

(d) If the pitcher makes an illegal pitch with the bases unoccupied, it shall be called a ball unless the batter reaches first base on a hit, an error, a base on balls, a hit batter or otherwise. A ball which slips out of the pitcher's hand and crosses the foul line shall be called a ball; otherwise it will be called "no pitch" without runners on base, and an illegal pitch (**A balk in Junior/Senior/Big League baseball**) with runners on base. (See Penalty for illegal pitch under Rule 8.05.)

(e) If the pitcher removes the pivot foot from contact with the pitcher's plate by stepping backward with that foot, that pitcher thereby becomes an infielder and in the case of a wild throw from that position, it shall be considered the same as a wild throw by any other infielder.

(f) **Tee Ball**: The pitcher shall keep both feet on the pitcher's plate until the ball is hit.

**8.02** - The pitcher shall not -

(a) (1) bring the pitching hand in contact with the mouth or lips while in the 10-foot circle (18-foot circle in **Junior/Senior/Big League baseball**) surrounding the pitcher's plate; **EXCEPTION: Provided it is agreed to by both managers, the umpire, prior to the start of a game played in cold weather, may permit the pitcher to blow on his/her hands while in the 10/18-foot circle.**

PENALTY: For violation of this part of the rule the umpires shall immediately call a ball and warn the pitcher that repeated violation of any part of this rule can cause the pitcher to be removed from the game. However, if the pitch is made and a batter reaches first base on a hit, an error, a hit batter or otherwise, and no other runner is put out before advancing at least one base, the play shall proceed without reference to the violation.

(2) apply a foreign substance of any kind to the ball;

(3) expectorate on the ball, either hand or the glove;

(4) rub the ball on the glove, person or clothing;

(5) deface the ball in any manner;

(6) deliver what is called the "shine" ball, "spit" ball, "mud" ball or "emery" ball. The pitcher is allowed to rub off the ball between the bare hands;

**PENALTY**: For violation of any part of this rule 8.02 (a), (2 through 6) the umpire shall: Call the pitch a ball and warn the pitcher.

If a play occurs on the violation, the manager of the offense may advise the plate umpire of acceptance of the play. (Such election must be made immediately at the end of play.)

**NOTE**: A pitcher may use a rosin bag for the purpose of applying rosin to the bare hand or hands. Neither the pitcher nor any other player shall dust the ball with the rosin bag; neither shall the pitcher nor any other player be permitted to apply rosin from the bag to their glove or dust any part of the uniform with the rosin bag.

(b) Intentionally delay the game by throwing the ball to players other than the catcher, when the batter is in position, except in an attempt to retire a runner, or commit an illegal pitch for the purpose of not pitching to the batter (i.e. intentional walk, etc...)
**PENALTY**: If, after warning by the umpire, such delaying action is repeated, the pitcher can be removed from the game.

(c) Intentionally pitch at the batter. If in the umpire's judgment, such violation occurs, the umpire shall warn the pitcher and the manager of the defense that another such pitch will mean immediate expulsion of the pitcher. If such pitch is repeated during the game, the umpire shall eject the pitcher from the game.

**8.03** - When a pitcher takes a position at the beginning of each inning, that pitcher shall be permitted to pitch not to exceed eight preparatory pitches to the catcher, or other teammate acting in the capacity of catcher, during which play shall be suspended. Such preparatory pitches shall not consume more than one minute of time. If a sudden emergency causes a pitcher to be summoned into the game without any opportunity to warm up, the umpire-in-chief shall allow the pitcher as many pitches as the umpire deems necessary.

**8.04** - When the bases are unoccupied, the pitcher shall deliver the ball to the batter within 20 seconds after the pitcher receives the ball. Each time the pitcher delays the game by violating this rule, the umpire shall call "Ball."

**NOTE**: The intent of this rule is to avoid unnecessary delays. The umpire shall insist that the catcher return the ball promptly to the pitcher, and that the pitcher take a position on the pitcher's plate promptly.

**8.05** - An illegal pitch (**A balk in Junior/Senior/Big League baseball**) when a runner or runners are on base is when -

(a) the pitcher, while touching the plate, makes any motion naturally associated with the pitch and fails to make such delivery;

(b) the pitcher, while touching the plate, feints a throw to first base and fails to complete the throw;

(c) the pitcher, while touching the plate, fails to step directly toward a base before throwing to that base;

(d) the pitcher, while touching the plate, throws, or feints a throw to an unoccupied base, except for the purpose of making a play;

(e) the pitcher makes a quick pitch; Umpires will judge a quick pitch as one delivered before the batter is reasonably set in the batter's box.
**NOTE**: A quick pitch is an illegal pitch. **Junior/Senior/Big League**: With runners on base penalty is a balk; with no runners on base, it is a ball. (See exceptions in "PENALTY.")

(f) the pitcher delivers the ball to the batter while not facing the batter;

(g) the pitcher makes any motion naturally associated with the pitch while not touching the pitcher's plate;

(h) the pitcher unnecessarily delays the game;

(i) the pitcher, without having the ball, stands on or astride the pitcher's plate or while off the plate feints a pitch;

(j) the pitcher, while touching the plate, accidentally or intentionally drops the ball;

(k)    the pitcher, while giving an intentional base on balls, pitches when the catcher is not in the catcher's box. In the situations noted above, in Little League (Majors) or Minor League, it is an illegal pitch even when runner(s) is/are not on base.

**NOTE**: There is no balk in Little League (Majors) or Minor League.
**PENALTY**: The pitch shall be called a ball. If a play follows the illegal pitch    the manager of the offense may advise the plate umpire of a decision to decline the illegal pitch penalty and accept the play. Such election shall be made immediately at the end of the play. However, if the batter hits the ball and reaches first base safely, and if all base-runners advance at least one base on the action resulting from the batted ball, the play proceeds without reference to the illegal pitch.
**NOTE**: A batter hit by a pitch shall be awarded first base without reference to the illegal pitch.

(l)    **Junior/Senior/Big League only**: The pitcher, after coming to a legal position, removes one hand from the ball other than in an actual pitch, or in throwing to a base;

(m)    **Junior/Senior/Big League only**: The pitcher delivers the pitch from the set position without coming to a stop.

**JUNIOR/SENIOR/BIG LEAGUE PENALTY**: The ball is dead, and each runner shall advance one base without liability to be put out unless the batter reaches first on a hit, an error, a base on balls, a hit batter or otherwise, and all other runners advance at least one base in which case the play proceeds without reference to the balk. When a balk is called and the pitch is delivered it will be considered neither a ball nor strike unless the pitch is ball four (4) awarding the batter first base and forcing all runners on base to advance. (**NOTE**: Umpires should bear in mind that the purpose of the balk rule is to prevent the pitcher from deliberately deceiving the base runner. If there is doubt in the umpire's mind, the "intent" of the pitcher should govern. However, certain specifics should be borne in mind:

(1)    Straddling the pitcher's plate without the ball is to be interpreted as intent to deceive and ruled a balk.

(2)    With a runner on first base, and the runner attempting to steal second, the pitcher may make a complete turn, without hesitating toward first, and throw to second. This is not to be interpreted as throwing to an unoccupied base.

**APPROVED RULING**: If the pitcher violates (a) through (m) in this rule and throws wild to a base, the runner or runners may advance at their own risk. (Delayed dead ball.)

**APPROVED RULING**: A runner who misses the first base to which that runner is advancing and who is called out on appeal shall be considered as having advanced one base for the purpose of this rule.

**8.06** - This rule, which applies to each pitcher who enters a game, governs the visits of the manager or coach to the pitcher **at the mound**.

(a)    A manager or coach may come out twice in one inning to visit with the pitcher, but the third time out, the player must be removed as a pitcher. Example: If a manager visits Pitcher A once in the first inning, then makes a pitching change in the same inning, Pitcher B would be allowed two visits in that inning before being removed on the third visit.

(b) A manager or coach may come out three times in one game to visit with the pitcher, but the fourth time out, the player must be removed as a pitcher. Example: If a manager visits Pitcher A twice in the first three innings, then makes a pitching change in the fourth inning, Pitcher B would be allowed three visits in that game before being removed on the fourth visit, subject to the limits in (a) above. (c)     The manager or coach is prohibited from making a third visit while the same batter is at bat.

(d) A manager or coach may confer with **any other player(s)**, including the catcher, during the visit with the pitcher. A manager or coach who is granted a time out to talk to any defensive player will be charged with a visit to the pitcher.

**APPROVED RULING 1**: At the time a pitcher is removed, a visit shall not be charged to the new pitcher.

**APPROVED RULING 2**: A conference with the pitcher or any other fielder to evaluate the player's condition after an injury shall not be considered a visit for the purposes of this rule. The manager or coach should advise the umpire of such a conference, and the umpire should monitor the conference.

## 9.00 - THE UMPIRE

**9.01** -

(a) The league president shall appoint one or more adult umpires to officiate at each league game. The umpire shall be responsible for the conduct of the game in accordance with these official rules and for maintaining discipline and order on the playing field during the game. Non-adult umpires may be used to supplement the umpire crew but the umpire-in-chief must always be an adult.

**NOTE**: Plate umpire must wear mask, shin guards and chest protector. Male umpire must wear protective cup. **NOTE**: It is highly recommended all umpires attach a "dangling" type throat protector to their mask.

(b) Each umpire is the representative of the league and of Little League Baseball, and is authorized and required to enforce all of these rules. Each umpire has authority to order a player, coach, manager or league officer to do or refrain from doing anything which affects the administering of these rules and to enforce the prescribed penalties.

(c) Each umpire has the authority to rule on any point not specifically covered in these rules.

(d) Each umpire has the authority to disqualify any player, coach, manager or substitute for objecting to the decisions or for unsportsmanlike conduct or language and to eject such disqualified person from the playing field. If an umpire disqualifies a player while a play is in progress, the disqualification shall not take effect until no further action is possible in that play.

(e) All umpires have the authority at their discretion to eject from the playing field (1) any person whose duties permit that person's presence on the field, such as ground crew members, photographers, newsmen, broadcasting crew members, etc. and (2) any spectator or other person not authorized to be on the playing field.

(f) Umpires may order both teams into their dugouts and suspend play until such time as League Officials deal with unruly spectators. Failure of League Officials to adequately handle an unruly spectator can result in the game remaining suspended until a later date.

**9.02 -**

(a) Any umpire's decision which involves judgment, such as, but not limited to, whether a batted ball is fair or foul, whether a pitch is a strike or a ball, or whether a runner is safe or out, is final. No player, manager, coach or substitute shall object to any such judgment decisions.

(b) If there is reasonable doubt that any umpire's decision may be in conflict with the rules, the manager may appeal the decision and ask that a correct ruling be made.
Such appeal shall be made only to the umpire who made the protested decision.

(c) If a decision is appealed, the umpire making the decision may ask another umpire for information before making a final decision. No umpire shall criticize, seek to reverse or interfere with another umpire's decision unless asked to do so by the umpire making it.

(d) No umpire may be replaced during a game unless injured or ill.

**9.03 -**

(a) If there is only one umpire, that umpire must be an adult and shall have complete jurisdiction in administering the rules. This umpire may take any position on the playing field which will enable said umpire to discharge all duties (usually behind the catcher, but sometimes behind the pitcher if there are runners.)

(b) If there are two or more umpires, one shall be designated umpire-in-chief and the others field umpires or a plate umpire.

(c) The umpire-in-chief may be a plate umpire or a field umpire. The umpire-in-chief's duties, in addition to any field or plate duties, shall be to:
(1) take full charge of, and be responsible for, the proper conduct of the game;
(2) make all decisions except those commonly reserved for the other field umpires or plate umpire;
(3) announce any special ground rules;

**9.04 -**

(a) The plate umpire shall stand behind the catcher. This umpire usually is designated as the umpire-in-chief. The plate umpire's duties shall be to:
(1) call and count balls and strikes;
(2) call and declare fair balls and fouls except those commonly called by field umpires;
(3) make all decision on the batter except those specifically reserved to the umpire-in-chief, or field umpire
(4) inform the official scorer of the official batting order; and any

changes in the lineups and batting order, on request.

(b) A field umpire may take any position (see Little League Umpire Manual) on the playing field best suited to make impending decisions on the bases. A field umpire's duties shall be to:

(1) make all decisions on the bases except those specifically reserved to the umpire-in-chief, or the plate umpire;

(2) take concurrent jurisdiction with the umpire-in-chief in calling "Time," illegal pitches, Junior/Senior/Big League balks, or defacement or discoloration of the ball by any player;

(3) aid the umpire-in-chief in every manner in enforcing the rules, excepting the power to forfeit the game, shall have equal authority with the umpire-in-chief in administering and enforcing the rules and maintaining discipline.

(c) If different decisions should be made on one play by different umpires, the umpire-in-chief shall call all the umpires into consultation, with no manager or player present. After consultation, the umpire-in-chief shall determine which decision shall prevail, based on which umpire was in the best position and which decision was most likely correct. Play shall proceed as if only the final decision had been made.

**9.05** -

(a) The umpire shall report to the league president within twenty-four hours after the end of a game all violations of rules and other incidents worthy of comment, including the disqualification of any manager, coach or player, and the reasons therefore.

(b) When any manager, coach or player is disqualified for a flagrant offense such as the use of obscene or indecent language, or an assault upon an umpire, manager, coach or player, the umpire shall forward full particulars to the league president within twenty-four hours after the end of the game.

(c) After receiving the umpire's report that a manager, coach or player has been disqualified, the league president shall require such manager, coach or player to appear before at least three members of the Board of Directors to explain their conduct. In the case of a player, the manager shall appear with the player in the capacity of an advisor. The members of the Board present at the meeting shall impose such penalty as they feel is justified. **NOTE**: The Board may impose such penalties that it feels are warranted, but may not lessen the requirements of Rule 4.07.

**9.06** - Umpires shall not wear shoes with metal spikes or cleats.

## IMPORTANT

Carry your Rule Book. It is better to consult the Rules and hold up the game long enough to decide a knotty problem than to have a game protested and possibly replayed.

## INDEX

5.02, 5.09, 5.10; When Live 3.12, 4.02, 5.01, 5.02, 5.11.

**Balls**: Official Game 1.09, 3.01 (c) (d) (e); Defacing, Discoloring 2.00 - Illegal Pitch, 3.02, 8.02 (a).

**Base Coaches**: Restrictions 4.05; Interference 4.05 (2 & 3), 7.09 (i-j), 5.08; Accidental Interference 5.08.

**Batter**: Becomes Runner 6.08, 6.09; Interference by 6.05 (g-h-j), 6.06 (c), 7.08 (g), 7.09; Out 6.02 (c), 6.05, 6.06, 6.07, 7.09, 7.11 - Penalty; Interference with 6.08 (c).

**Batter's Box**: 2.00, 1.04, 6.03, 6.06 (b).

**Batting Order**: 4.01, 4.04, 6.01-6.04.

**Batting Out of Order**: 6.07.

**Casts**: 1.11 (k).

**Catcher**: Interference by 6.08 (c); Interference with 5.09 (b), 6.06 (c), 7.08 (g).Position of: 4.03 (a).

**Defacing, Discoloring Ball**: 3.02 & 8.02 (a-5).

**Definitions**: 2.00.

**Deflected Batted Ball**: 6.09 (f-g), 7.05 (a-f).

**Delay of Game**: by Batter 6.02 (c); by Pitcher 8.02 (b), 8.04; Forfeit for Delays 4.15.

Discipline of Team Personnel: 3.02, 3.14, 4.05-4.08, 4.15, 8.02 (a-l), 8.02 (b-c), 9.01 (b-d), 9.05.

**Double-Headers**: 3.11, 4.12, 4.13.

**Equipment**: Athletic Supporter/Cup 1.17; Ball 1.09; Bases 1.04, 1.06; Bats 1.10; Benches/ Dugouts 1.08, 2.00-Bench; Chest Protector 1.17; Gloves 1.12, 1.13, 1.14, 1.15; Helmets 1.16, 1.17; Home Base 1.04, 1.05; Masks 1.17; Removed from Game - 4.19 (a), 1.10; Not Left Lying on field 3.14; Observance of all Rules Governing - 3.01 (a); Pitcher's Plate/Mound 1.04, 1.07; Shoes & Toe Plates 1.11 (g-h), 9.06; Throat Protector 1.17; Thrown at Ball: 7.05 (a-c-e); Uniforms 1.11.

**Fair Ball**: 2.00; Bounces Out of Play 6.09 (f-g), 7.05 (f).

**Fielder in Dead Ball Area**: 5.10 (f), 7.04 (b).

**Fielder's Choice**: 2.00.

**Forfeited Game**: 2.00, 4.15, 4.16, 4.17, 4.18.

**Ground Rules**: 3.13, 9.04 (a-8)

**Illegal Pitch**: 2.00, Caused by catcher 4.03 (a), Caused by Offensive Team 4.06 (3); Ball Dead 5.09 (c), 8.01 (d), 8.02 (a-6), 8.05; Penalty 8.05; Penalty Waived 8.05.

**Illegally Batted Ball**: 2.00, 5.09 (d), 6.03, 6.06 (a).

**Infield Fly**: 2.00, 6.05 (d) & (k) - Note, 7.08 (f) - Exception & Note.

**Intentionally Dropped Ball**: 6.05 (k).

**Interference**: Defensive 2.00 (b), 6.08 (c); Offensive 2.00 (a), 5.09 (f), 6.05 (g-h-j-l), 6.06 (c), 6.08 (d), 6.09 (b), 7.08 (b-f-g), 7.09, 7.11; Spectator 2.00 (d), 3.16, 3.18; Umpire 2.00 (c), 5.09 (b-f), 6.08 (d), 6.09 (b), 7.04 (b).

**Jewelry**: 1.11 (j).

**Lights & Light Failure**: 4.12, 4.14, 5.10 (b-h).

**Mandatory Play**: Regulation IV (i).

**Missed Base**: 7.02, 7.04 - Note, 7.08 (k), 7.10 (b), 7.12, 8.05 - Penalty - Approved Ruling #2.

**Obstruction**: 2.00, 7.06.

**Official Scorer**: See "What's the Score" publication.

**Overrunning First Base**: 7.08 (c & j), 7.10 (c).

**Pitcher**: May Not Re-enter Game as Pitcher 3.03 - Note 1; Shall Pitch to First Batter 3.05; Warming up 3.09; Pitching in Resumption of Game 4.11 (e) - Note, 4.12; Legal Positions 8.01 (a) (b); Becomes Infielder 8.01 (e); Takes Signs While on Pitcher's plate 8.01; Throws out of play 7.05 (h); Throws to a Base 8.01 (c); Throws at Batter 8.02 (c); Preparatory Pitches 8.03; Visits by Manager or Coach to 8.06.

**Player's Position**: 4.03.

**Playing Field**: 1.04, See Diagrams of Field Layout and Batter's Boxes.

**Postponement/Suspension Responsibilities**: 3.10, 4.01.

**Protested Games**: 4.19.**Regulation Games**: 4.10, 4.11.

**Resuming Play After Dead Ball**: 5.11.

**Restrictions on Players**: No Fraternizing 3.09; Barred from Stands 3.09; Confined to Bench 3.17.

**Runner**: Advance of 7.04; 7.05; 7.06; Entitled to Base 7.01, 7.03; Base Touching Requirements 7.02; 7.04 - Note, 7.08 (d) (k), 7.10 (a) (b) (d), 7.12; Is Out 5.08, 5.09 (f), 7.08-7.11; Leaving Early 7.13; Reverse Run Prohibited 7.08 (i); Running Out of Baseline 7.08 (a-l).

**Score of Games**: 4.09 (b), 4.11.

**Scoring Rules**: See "What's the Score" Publication.

**Scoring Runs**: 4.09, 4.11, 5.02, 5.06, 5.10 (c), 6.09 (c) (g), 7.02, 7.05 (a), 7.12.

**Spectators**: Barred from Field 3.15, 3.18; Touching Batted or Thrown Ball 3.16; Actions Causing Dispute 4.19 Note 1; Not Mingling with 3.09.

**Strike**: 2.00.

**Strike Zone**: 2.00, 6.02, 6.08 (b).

**Substitutions**: 3.03-3.08; 4.04, 4.08, 4.12, 5.10 (c).

**Ten Run Rule**: 4.10 (e).

**Tie Games**: 4.11 (e), 4 12.

**Umpires**: 9.00.

**Unsportsmanlike Conduct**: 4.06, 9.01 (d).

**Wild Throws**: 5.08, 7.05 (g-h-i).

**Policy Statement: Little Leaguers on Television, Radio, and the Internet**

Little League International in South Williamsport, Pa., is the only body that can authorize or disallow the webcasting, televising or radio broadcasting of any game(s). A contract (provided by Little League International) must originate with the local District Administrator, tournament director or local Little League president. (See Regulation XV.)

No telecast, broadcast or webcast of any Little League Baseball or Softball game (in any division) can take place unless the proper contract is completed and approved. This applies to all productions, even if they are unsupported by advertising, sponsorship or subscriptions.

To download a contract for games below the Regional level, visit www.Little-League.org/media.htm

For contracts at the Regional and World Series tournament levels, contact the Little League International Publicity Department in South Williamsport at 570-326-1921, Ext. 238; or write to the Director of Publicity, Chris Downs, at cdowns@LittleLeague.org

For local leagues, districts and media personnel, Little League International has guidelines regarding the appearance of Little Leaguers in newspapers, on television, in magazines, etc. To download a PDF file of the document, visit www.LittleLeague.org/media.htm

## 2010 Tournament Rules and Guidelines for
## Little League Baseball
## 9-10 Year Old Division Baseball, 10-11 Year Old Division,
## Junior League, Senior League and Big League Baseball

### Points of Emphasis in Bold Italic

Tournament play started in Little League in 1947. Conduct of tournament play by District Administrators began in 1956 following the first Little League International Congress. Today, responsibility for scheduling and supervising all district tournament games comes under jurisdiction of the District Administrator. Headquarters has the right to appoint Tournament Directors at other levels of tournament play.

The Tournaments of Little League have grown year by year until today they have become the outstanding, in fact, the only exposure that the majority of the public sees. In many cases, they are the criterion by which Little League is judged. Proper conduct at tournament time imposes a large responsibility upon all concerned. Good judgment and exemplary disciplines are demanded if Little League tournaments of the future are to remain worthwhile in the public esteem.

The Little League Baseball Tournament, 9-10 Year Old Division Baseball Tournament, 10-11 Year Old Division Baseball Tournament, Junior League, Senior League and Big League Baseball Tournaments are authorized by the Board of Directors. Leagues which exercise the option to participate in Tournament Play must pledge they will do so with full knowledge of the rules and in agreement that the rules will be upheld.

**Rules**: Except where noted in these Tournament Rules and Guidelines, the Little League Baseball Official Regulations and Playing Rules will be used in the conduct of the 9-10 Year Old Division Tournament, the 10-11 Year old Division Tournament, the Little League Baseball Tournament, Junior League, Senior League and Big League Baseball Tournaments.

**9-10 Year Old Division & 10-11 Year Old Division**: The objective of the 9-10 Year Old Division & 10-11 Year Old Division Tournament is to provide nine and ten year old players, and ten and eleven year old players, the opportunity to participate in a baseball tournament at the District, Sectional, and State levels at the conclusion of the regular season. Leagues are strongly encouraged to place the maximum number of players (14) on the Tournament Affidavit, thereby giving more children the opportunity to participate.

### Responsibility and Chain of Command

It should be clearly understood by Tournament Directors and league presidents that operation of the annual tournaments in Little League come under a different authority and jurisdiction from that normally observed during the playing season. It is, in fact, a whole new ball game. Once the tournament season starts, authority is vested solely in the Tournament Committee at Williamsport.

There will be no waivers or resorting to local rules or other variation unless granted explicitly from Williamsport. To administer the tournament properly and scale down thousands of teams to two finalists in the limited time afforded by the tournament season is an undertaking requiring considerable disciplines. Once the tournament starts, it must proceed without interruption. If protests or disputes occur which cannot be settled by the umpires or Tournament Director through immediate and concise application of the rules, an appeal must be made through proper channels promptly to prevent a major blockage or loss of momentum.

Revocation of tournament privileges or forfeiture of a tournament game may be decided only by the Tournament Committee at Williamsport. Should a problem arise that cannot be resolved while a game is in progress, the game must be suspended by the umpire-in-chief and the problem referred immediately to the Tournament Director. If not resolved, it must be referred to the Regional Director. If still unresolved, it will be referred to the Tournament Committee in Williamsport. If the Tournament Committee deems any player to be ineligible, by league age, residency, participation in other programs, or participation in less than sixty (60) percent the regular season games, it may result in forfeiture of tournament game(s), and/or suspension or removal of personnel from tournament play, and/or suspension or removal of personnel or teams from further Little League activities, and/or suspension or revocation of the local league's charter. These actions can only be taken by the Tournament Committee in Williamsport.

The Tournament Committee and the individual Regional Directors may appoint agents to act on their behalf, and any person so appointed shall have the authority to act as, and exercise the duties of, the Tournament Committee or the individual Regional Directors.

The Tournament Committee also reserves the right to impose any of the above penalties if, in its judgment, any player, manager or coach displays unsportsmanlike conduct during the game, at the game site, or at any event related to the International Tournament. The committee also reserves the right to impose any penalty the committee deems appropriate, if the committee determines action is necessary to correct a situation brought to its attention, regardless of the source of that information. The decision of the Tournament Committee is final and binding.

Knowledge of the rules must be guaranteed before a Tournament Director is declared qualified. All Tournament Directors will undergo a thorough and instructive briefing session prior to taking on their duties, must signify that they understand the rules and regardless of personal feelings, they are in full agreement and can interpret them properly. At the time of the district tournament meeting, it will be required that each league president or the representative in attendance signify that the league and tournament team managing personnel are knowledgeable of Tournament Rules and are in full agreement with these conditions.

## Selection of Tournament Teams (Recommended Method)

Little League would gain immeasurably in esteem of the public if all tournament teams were selected by the players themselves. Players relish the challenge of competition, but their anxiety to excel is in balance with an intuitive respect and admiration for teammate and opponent alike who demonstrate superior ability and skill. The Tournament Committee also reserves the right to impose any of the above penalties if, in its judgment, any player, manager or coach displays unsportsmanlike conduct during the game, at the site or at any event related to the International Tournament. *The committee also reserves the right to impose any penalty the committee deems appropriate if in the committees determines action is necessary to correct a situation brought to its attention regardless of the source of that information. The decision of the Tournament Committee is final and binding.*

1. It is not required that players be selected for the position they occupy during the regular season. For example, a pitcher who is also a good outfielder or infielder may be placed on the roster and used in whatever position the manager deems to be of advantage.

2. Tournament team candidates should be selected upon their playing ability and eligibility. The roster should include sufficient pitching strength to meet tournament schedules.

3. The following plan was presented to the International Congress, Washington, D.C., 1965, as a guideline, taken from the experience of the International Advisory Council. The principle is to have all components of a league determine and participate in fair and democratic selection of the tournament team. This would eliminate many of the complaints, abuses, pressures and charges of favoritism which are directed toward the league president. The following groups should each select its tournament team.

   Group 1 - Players
   Group 2 - League Officers
   Group 3 - Team Managers
   Group 4 - Team Coaches
   Group 5 - Volunteer Umpires

Every player on the eligible teams is entitled to vote. Each group submits its list of players at a meeting of the Board of Directors of the league. The names are to be read and counted from each of the groups, and the players in the order of total votes received will become eligible for the tournament team. Where more than one player has an equal number of votes to qualify for the last position or positions, final selection should be made by a majority vote of the Board of Directors at the time of the meeting.

**NOTE: Method of selection is to be determined by the Local League Board of Directors.**

## TOURNAMENT ORGANIZATION

**Teams**

Each chartered league shall be eligible to enter a team. Alternates are not authorized.

(**NOTE**: In the 9-10 Year Old Division and 10-11 Year Old Division, a league may enter more than one tournament team with the District Administrator's approval.)

Where two or more charters have combined to form a single program, a tournament team must be selected for each charter composed of players from within its own chartered area. Exceptions can only be made by the Charter Committee.

Tournament teams and Eligibility Affidavit shall consist of, and must be limited to, a maximum of fourteen (14) players, one (1) manager and a maximum of two (2) coaches. If there are thirteen (13) or more eligible players listed on the team's affidavit, the maximum of three (3) adults shall be listed on the affidavit; if a tournament team has twelve (12) or fewer eligible players listed on the team affidavit, the maximum of two (2)adults shall be listed on the affidavit.

**Senior League:** Teams and Eligibility Affidavit shall consist of, and must be limited to, a maximum of sixteen (16) players, one (1) manager and a maximum of two (2) coaches.

**Big League:** Tournament teams may be selected from all league teams in a district or may be a regular season unit team. Teams and Eligibility Affidavit shall consist of, and must be limited to, a maximum of seventeen (17) players, one (1) manager and a maximum of two (2) coaches.

## Managers and Coaches

The president of the League, the District Administrator or District Staff shall not serve as manager or coach.

**Little League**: The manager and coach (es) shall be regular season team managers and/or coaches from the Little League Baseball (Majors) Division.

**9-10 Division & 10-11 Year Old Division**: The manager and coach (es) shall be regular season team managers and/or coaches from the Little League Baseball (Majors) Division or Minor League Division.

**Junior League**: The manager and coach(es) shall be regular season team managers and/or coaches from the Junior Division or Senior Division.

**Senior League**: The manager and coach(es) shall be regular season team managers and/or coaches from the Junior Division, Senior Division or Big League Division.

**Big League**: The manager and coach (es) shall be regular season team managers and/or coaches from the Senior Division or Big League Division.

**Managers/Coaches in the Dugout** - If a tournament team has thirteen (13) or more eligible players in uniform at a game, then the maximum of three (3) persons who are named on the affidavit (or authorized temporary replacements as noted on the affidavit) as manager/coaches will be permitted to act as manager/coaches for that game. However, if a tournament team has twelve (12) or fewer eligible players in uniform at a game, then a maximum of two (2) persons must be named at the start of the game as manager and coach. The two named persons must be listed on the affidavit as manager/coach, or must be authorized temporary replacements as noted on the affidavit. If there is a third person listed on the affidavit asa manager/coach, that person is not permitted to be in the dugout or on the field during that game. **Note.** The manager, temporary manager or substitute manager must be an adult. See Rule 2.00 (BASE COACH and COACH).

## Umpires

The Tournament Director shall have full responsibility for providing volunteer Little League umpires for tournament play. Umpires from leagues involved in the game should not be assigned. The District Administrator shall not umpire.

There should be at least two umpires in each game. More are recommended when available.

The designated Umpire-in-Chief for each game must be an adult.

**Tournament Eligibility Affidavit**

It shall be the league president's responsibility to review and certify the birth records (league age) by viewing the original birth record and residence (as defined by Little League Baseball, Incorporated) of all players. When the league finally decides on the makeup of the team, names must be entered on the league's Eligibility Affidavit. Once the District Administrator certifies the eligibility affidavit, the tournament team will be required to have in its possession:

1.  the tournament affidavit;
2.  copies (originals not required) of the records used to verify date of birth for all players on the affidavit;
3.  a map showing the actual boundaries of the league, with locations noted for the residences of the parent or legal guardian (court appointed) of every participant named on the affidavit.
4.  three or more documents to determine residency of the parent(s) or guardian for each player named on the tournament affidavit.
5.  **waivers (i.e. II(d), IV(h), Charter Committee, etc...)**

**IMPORTANT: Alternates are not authorized. They shall not accompany the team and shall not be listed on the Eligibility Affidavit.**

Eligibility Affidavit must be certified by the District Administrator or his or her designated appointee and presented by the team manager to the Tournament Director before every game. NOTE: The Eligibility Affidavit becomes official once the team plays its first tournament game.

**Participation In Other Programs**

Participation in other programs during the International Tournament is permitted, subject to the provisions of Regulation IV (a) Note 2.

**Release of Names**

**Little League, Junior/Senior/Big League**: The release of names of players selected for the tournament team shall not be made before June 15 and not until the availability and eligibility of all prospective team members have been established. (Little League accident insurance for Tournament Teams will not go into effect until June 15, or the announcement of Tournament Team members, whichever is later).

**9-10 Year Old Division and 11 Year Old Division**: The release of names of players selected for the tournament team shall not be made before June 15, or two weeks prior to the start of the tournament (whichever is earlier), and not until the availability and eligibility of all prospective team members have been established. (Little League accident insurance for tournament teams will not go into effect until June 15, or the date of the release of the names of Tournament Team members, whichever is earlier).

**Violation of this rule may be cause for revocation of tournament privilege by the Tournament Committee.**

## League Eligibility

In order for a Little League program to be eligible to enter a team or teams into the International Tournament (including 9-10 Year Old Division and 10-11 Year Old Division) the following must be accomplished as indicated:

1) The league must be chartered in the division(s) for which it wishes to enter a tournament team(s), no later than June 8, 2010. Examples: Chartered in Little League Majors to enter a Major Division team (11-12 year olds); chartered in Senior League to enter a Senior Division team, etc.

2) The league must have scheduled and played, at a minimum, a 12-game (per team) regular season exclusive of playoffs and tournament games for each division entering tournament. See Reg. VII. The schedule shall be arranged so that at least one-half of the games are scheduled prior to June 15.

3) All waivers requests (for the league, team, player, manager, and/or coach) of any kind must be submitted and approved not later than June 8, 2010.

4) All regular season team rosters must be submitted to Little League International in accordance with the requirements outlined in Regulation IV (g), not later than June 8, 2010;

5) Team number revisions and fees incurred by the league must be paid in full by June 8, 2010.

6) All combined team and interleague play requests that may involve tournament play must be submitted and approved not later than June 8, 2010.

Failure to meet any of the listed requirements could result in a team or teams being declared ineligible by the Tournament Committee at Little League International.

## Player Eligibility

Players are eligible for Tournament Play, provided they meet the criteria established by the Little League "Residency Eligibility Requirement," "Participation In Other Programs" and the following:

**Little League (Majors Division)** - Any player League Age 11 or 12, who has participated as an eligible player in 60 percent the regular season games as of June 15 on a Little League Baseball (Majors Division) team, with the exception of the school baseball season.

**9-10 Year Old Division** - Any player League Age 9 or 10, who has participated as an eligible player in 60 percent the regular season games as of June 15, with the exception of the school baseball season, on a:

1. Little League Baseball (Majors Division) team, or;
2. Minor League Baseball team.

**10-11 Year old Division - Any player League Age 10 or 11, who has participated as an eligible player in 60 percent the regular season games as of June 15, with the exception of the school baseball season, on a:**

1. **Little League Baseball (Majors Division) team, or;**
2. **Minor League Baseball team.**

**Big League** - Any player League Age 16, 17 or 18, with amateur status, who has been a rostered member for 60 percent the regular season games (special games may be counted toward this requirement) by the start of Tournament Play in their respective District, with the exception of the high school or college baseball season, on a:

1. Big League Baseball Team, or;
2. Senior League Baseball Team.

**Senior League** - Any player League Age 14, 15 or 16, with amateur status, who has participated as an eligible player in 60 percent the regular season games as of June 15, with the exception of the middle school, junior high school or high school baseball season, on a:

1. Big League Baseball Team, or;
2. Senior League Baseball Team, or;
3. Junior League Baseball Team.

**Junior League** - Any player League Age 12-14, who has participated as an eligible player in 60 percent the regular season games as of June 15, with the exception of the middle school, junior high school or high school baseball season, on a:

1. Senior League Baseball Team, or;
2. Junior League Baseball Team.

**NOTE 1**: Consistent with a manager's ability to conduct the affairs of his or her team, a manager may disqualify a player from the team for the current season, subject to Board of Directors approval, if the player repeatedly misses practice or games.

**NOTE 2**: The Big League Baseball, Senior League Baseball and Junior League Baseball Tournaments are divided by age, without regard to the regular season division in which a player participates, as noted above.

**CONDITION 1**: Participation must be within the chartered league named on the Eligibility Affidavit.

**CONDITION 2**: A player who is not able to participate in a number of local league regular season games because of participation in a school baseball program will receive an adjustment on the minimum participation in games required under this rule.

**Example**: If, for any given division, Team A played 20 regular season games before June 15, and a player missed 10 games because of participation in a school baseball program, that player is required to have participated in only six (6) regular season games to be eligible for the Tournament Team.

**CONDITION 3:** A player may be named to the roster of, and practice with, only ONE Little League International Tournament Team. Once the affidavit is signed by the local league president, player agent and District Administrator (or their representatives), the players listed on the affidavit shall not be eligible to participate on any other Little League International Tournament Team for the current year.

**Baseball players league age 10, 11, 14, and 16 may be eligible for selection to multiple tournament teams. These players may only be selected to one tournament team. Under no circumstances may these players be chosen for, practice with or participate with more than one tournament team.**

*Violation of this rule may be cause for revocation of tournament privilege*

## Tournament Requirement for Non-Citizens

A participant who is not a citizen of the country in which he/she wishes to play, but meets residency requirements as defined by Little League, may participate in that country if:

1. his/her visa allows that participant to remain in that country for a period of at least one year, or;
2. the prevailing laws allow that participant to remain in that country for at least one year, or;
3. the participant has an established bona fide residence in that country for at least two years prior to the start of the regular season.

Exceptions can only be made by action of the Charter Committee in Williamsport.

## Insurance

Accident: A league or District Big League team shall not be accepted for tournament play unless covered by accident insurance, which includes tournament play. It is strongly recommended that a medical release for each player on the Affidavit be carried by the team manager.

Liability: Liability Insurance must be carried by the league on whose field tournaments are played as well as all leagues who participate in the tournament. Minimum coverage of $1,000,000 single limit, bodily injury and property damage. The policy must include coverage for claims arising out of athletic participants.

*If insurance is purchased locally, a copy of the policy must be on file at Little League Baseball International.*

## Replacement of Player, Manager or Coach

Any player, manager or coach listed on the Eligibility Affidavit who is unable to participate because of injury, illness, vacation or other justifiable reason may be replaced by another eligible person. If a player, manager or coach is replaced, that person may not be returned to the Tournament Affidavit. Permanent replacements must be from the league's regular season teams and shall be recorded and approved by the District Administrator or Tournament Director in the space provided on the Eligibility Affidavit. Exception: If a manager or coach is unable to attend a game for a justifiable reason, a Tournament Director could approve a temporary replacement. Temporary replacement of a manager or coach need not be entered on the Eligibility Affidavit. **A manager or coach who is ejected from a game may not be replaced for the team's next physically played game. (See Rule 4.07)**

## Playing Equipment

The dimensions and other specifications of all playing equipment used must conform to those set forth in the Official Little League, Junior League, Senior League, Big League Baseball Playing Rules except for those noted below:

Every member of the team must wear a conventional uniform which includes shirt, pants, stockings and cap. This may be a regular season uniform.

Each team must provide at least six (6) (7 for **Junior/Senior/Big League Baseball**) NOCSAE approved safety helmets with warning labels. The batter, all base runners, (on-deck batter for **Junior/Senior/Big League baseball**) and player base coaches must wear approved helmets.

All male players must wear athletic supporters. Catchers (male) must wear the metal, fibre or plastic type cup.

Catchers must wear a mask with (NOCSAE) approved catchers helmet (**skull cap type not acceptable**) and "dangling" type throat guard during practice, infield/outfield, pitcher warm-up and games. All catchers must wear approved chest protector and shin guards. Male catchers must wear long model chest protector with neck collar. **Junior/Senior/Big League**:  Catchers must wear approved long or short model chest protectors.

Shoes with metal cleats or spikes shall not be worn by players, managers, coaches or umpires. **Junior/Senior/Big League**: Players may wear shoes with metal spikes.

## Schedules

Each District Administrator must finalize tournament schedules prior to the start of the tournament or June 15 (whichever is earliest).  Schedules for each level (District, Section, Division, State, Regional) must utilize Little League Baseball approved single elimination brackets, double elimination brackets, or pool play format with pool play tie breaker format, as noted beginning on Page T-26. All other tournament formats must be approved by the Tournament Committee.

**9-10 & 10-11 Year Old Division/Little League**: A team may play two games in one day with the approval of the Regional Director.

**Junior/Senior/Big League**: Teams may participate in a maximum of two (2) games in a day.

**NOTE 1**: Inclement weather may be justification to revert to single elimination in order to complete a tournament on schedule, with the approval of the Regional Director.

**NOTE 2**: The 9-10 & 10-11 Year Old Divisions advances to state level only.

**NOTE 3**: Consult approved schedules for specific dates. Tournament dates may vary.

## Tournament Team Practice

**Little League Baseball, Junior/Senior/Big League Baseball**: Try-outs or practices by tournament teams shall not be held before June 15. Tournament team practice may only take place against other players in the same league and division, providing such practice is done out of uniform. (Little League accident insurance for tournament teams will not go into effect until June 15, or the date of the release of the names of Tournament Team members, whichever is later).

**9-10 & 10-11 Year Old Divisions**: Try-outs or practices by tournament teams shall not be held before June 15, or two weeks prior to the start of the tournament, whichever is earlier. Tournament team practice may only take place against other players in the same league, providing such practice is done out of uniform. (Little League accident insurance for tournament teams will not go into effect until June 15, or the date of the release of the names of Tournament Team members, whichever is earlier). *Violation of this rule may be cause for revocation of tournament privileges by the Tournament Committee.*

## Selection of Fields

All games shall be played upon Little League fields approved by the Tournament Director. Exception to this rule can only be made with the consent of the Regional Director.

Fields must be enclosed with an outfield fence. Outfield fences for the Little League Division must be a maximum of 225 feet from home plate and a minimum of 195 feet; for 9-10 and 10-11 divisions, a maximum of 225 feet and a minimum of 180 feet; for Junior League, a maximum of 350 feet and a minimum of 250 feet; for Senior League and Big League, a maximum of 420 feet and a minimum of 280 feet. Tournament Directors should not permit portable outfield fences to exceed 200 feet (300 feet for **Junior/Senior/Big League Baseball**). Conventional dirt mounds are approved for tournament play. A request to use an artificial mound for tournament play may be submitted to the Tournament Committee in Williamsport (through the District Administrator/Tournament Director and Regional Office). An artificial mound must not be used unless approved in writing by the Tournament Committee for a specific tournament site/level, and only for the current year. The Tournament Director or assistant shall judge fitness of the playing field before the game starts.

**9-10 & 10-11 Year Old Divisions, Little League**: The on-deck batter's position is not permitted.

**NOTE:** For additional information about field selection see "Physical Conditions" on Page T-22.

## Games Under Lights

Games under lights may be scheduled at all levels of tournament play. The District Administrator having jurisdiction must determine that lighting installations meet minimum standards approved by Little League Headquarters.

## Curfew

No inning shall start after 11:00 p.m. (11:30 p.m. for **Junior/Senior League Baseball**; midnight for **Big League Baseball**) prevailing time. **NOTE**: An inning starts the moment the third out is made completing the previous inning.

## Starting Time of Games

A game shall not be started unless the Tournament Director or assistant judges there is adequate time to complete the game before darkness or curfew.

## Admission Charge

There shall be no charge for admission to Little League Tournament, 9-10 or 11 Year Old Divisions Tournament games. An admission charge is permitted for Junior/Senior/Big League Baseball.

# CONDITIONS OF TOURNAMENT PLAY

## Protests

This rule replaces Rule 4.19.

No protest shall be considered on a decision involving an umpire's judgment. Equipment which does not meet specifications must be removed from the game.

**Protest shall be considered only when based on:**

A. **The violation or interpretation of a playing rule;**
   When a manager claims that a decision is in violation of the playing rules, the following steps must be taken:
   1. A formal (verbal) protest must be made to the umpire-in-chief at once by the manager or coach.
   2. The umpire-in-chief must immediately call a conference of all umpires working the game.
   3. If the problem cannot be resolved to the satisfaction of the managers, the umpire-in-chief shall be required to consult with the Tournament Director or District Administrator.
   4. If the managers do not accept the decision of the Tournament Director, either manager may elect, without penalty, to discontinue play until the matter is referred to the Regional Headquarters. Either the umpire-in-chief, Tournament Director or District Administrator will call the Regional Headquarters at this time.
   5. If the managers do not accept the decision of the Regional Director (or his/her designated agent), either may insist that the matter be referred to the Tournament Committee in Williamsport. The decision of the Tournament Committee shall be final and binding.

   **NOTE 1** - PROTESTS INVOLVING PLAYING RULES NOT RESOLVED BEFORE THE NEXT PITCH OR PLAY SHALL NOT BE CONSIDERED.
   **NOTE 2** - UMPIRES, TOURNAMENT DIRECTORS AND DISTRICT ADMINISTRATORS DO NOT HAVE THE AUTHORITY TO DECLARE A FORFEITURE UNDER ANY CIRCUMSTANCES.
   **NOTE 3** - PROTESTS BECAUSE OF A TEAM'S FAILURE TO MEET THE MANDATORY PLAY REQUIREMENTS (SEE TOURNAMENT RULE 9) MUST BE MADE BEFORE THE UMPIRE(S) LEAVE THE PLAYING FIELD. NOTE: MANDATORY PLAY DOES NOT APPLY TO THE SENIOR LEAGUE AND BIG LEAGUE DIVISIONS.

B. **The use of an ineligible pitcher;**
   Ineligibility under this rule applies to violations of Tournament Playing Rule 4. If an ineligible pitcher delivers one or more pitches to a batter, that game may be subject to protest and action by the Tournament Committee in Williamsport, subject to the following conditions:
   1. At any time before the umpire(s) leave the playing field, a formal (verbal) protest must be made to the umpire-in-chief by the manager or coach.

2. The umpire-in-chief must immediately consult with the Tournament Director or District Administrator.
3. Either the umpire-in-chief, Tournament Director or District Administrator will call the Regional Headquarters at this time.
4. The Regional Director (or his/her designated agent) will contact the Tournament Committee in Williamsport. The decision of the Tournament Committee shall be final and binding. **NOTE**: The Manager is responsible for verifying the accuracy of the pitching record on the eligibility affidavit.

C. **The use of an ineligible player.**
Ineligibility under this rule applies to league age, residence (as defined by Little League Baseball, Incorporated), participation in other programs, participation as an eligible player for sixty (60) percent of the regular season in the proper division or a violation of Regulations I-XVII.
1. If the facts establishing or verifying the ineligibility of a player are known to the complainant **PRIOR TO** the game, the following steps must be taken:
   (a) The complainant shall present the matter to the Tournament Director and/or District Administrator.
   (b) The matter **SHALL** be resolved with the Regional Director and, through the Regional Director and the Tournament Committee **BEFORE** the first pitch of the game. The decision of the Tournament Committee shall be final and binding.
2. If the facts establishing or verifying the ineligibility of a player become known **DURING** a game, and the ineligible player participates in the game, that team shall forfeit the game in question, subject to the following conditions:
   (a) A protest may be lodged by the manager or coach with the umpire-in-chief, who shall consult with the Tournament Director or District Administrator.
   (b) The Tournament Director or District Administrator must contact the Regional Director (or his/her appointed agent), who shall contact the Tournament Committee for a decision. The decision of the Tournament Committee shall be final and binding.
3. If the facts establishing or verifying the ineligibility of a player become known **AFTER** a game, and the ineligible player participated in the game, that team shall forfeit the game in question, subject to the following conditions:
   (a) A protest may be lodged by the manager or coach with the Tournament Director or District Administrator. Such protest must be made before either team affected by the protest begins another game.
   (b) The Tournament Director or District Administrator must contact the Regional Director (or his/her appointed agent), who shall contact the Tournament Committee for a decision. The decision of the Tournament Committee shall be final and binding.

**NOTE 1**: Disqualification of a team or player(s) and/or forfeiture of a game must be the decision of the Tournament Committee at Williamsport, and such decisions will be made prior to the continuation of the affected team(s) or player(s) in further tournament play.

**NOTE 2**: All officials, including all managers, coaches, scorekeepers, umpires, Tournament Directors, District Administrators, etc., should make every effort to prevent a situation that may result in the forfeiture of a game or suspension of tournament privileges. However, failure by any party to prevent such situations shall not affect the validity of a protest.

**Must Play To Advance**

A team shall not advance from one level of Tournament to a higher level of tournament play without first having competed against and defeated a scheduled opponent at the tournament level from which it is seeking to advance. Any team advancing without play must do so with the approval of the Regional Director.

## TOURNAMENT PLAYING RULES

The Official Little League, Junior League, Senior League and Big League Baseball Playing Rules shall govern tournament play except as noted below:

1. **BASEBALLS**: Baseballs licensed by Little League with the "RS-T" (regular season and tournament) designation must be used.

2. **FIELDS**: All fields are considered neutral. The home team shall be determined by the toss of a coin, the winner having the choice.

3. **PLAYING RULES**: A copy of the Official Little League Junior League, Senior League and Big League Baseball Regulations and Playing Rules and the Tournament Rules and Guidelines must be available at each tournament site and at the time the game is to be played. This is the responsibility of the Tournament Director. Written ground rules established by the Tournament Director or assistant must be reviewed with both managers and umpire-in-chief at least ten (10) minutes before the start of the game. It is suggested the same be available to news media if requested.

### 4. PITCHING RULES – LITTLE LEAGUE BASEBALL, 9-10 YEAR OLD, 10-11 YEAR OLD DIVISION, AND JUNIOR LEAGUE

These rules replace the regular season pitching regulations. *Violation of these pitching rules is subject to protest and action by the Tournament Committee in Williamsport if protested before the umpire(s) leave the playing field.*

a. Any player on a tournament team may pitch. (**NOTE : There is no limit to the number of pitchers a tournament team may use in a game.**)

b. A tournament pitcher may not pitch in regular season or Special Games while the team is still participating in the tournament.

c. Pitchers once removed from the mound may not return as pitchers **Junior/Senior League**: A pitcher remaining in the game, but moving to a different position,can return as a pitcher anytime in the remainder of the game, but only once per game.

d. The manager must remove the pitcher when said pitcher reaches the limit for his/her age group as noted below, but the pitcher may remain in the game at another position:

League Age:  13 -14   95 pitches per day
             11 -12   85 pitches per day
             9-10     75 pitches per day

**EXCEPTION**: If a pitcher reaches the limit imposed above for his/her league age while facing a batter, the pitcher may continue to pitch until any one of the following conditions occurs: 1. That batter reaches base; 2. That batter is put out; 3. The third out is made to complete the half-inning. **(Note: A pitcher who delivers 41 or more pitches in a game cannot play the postion of catcher for the remainder of that day.)**

e. Pitchers league age 14 and under must adhere to the following rest requirements:

• If a player pitches 66 or more pitches in a day, four (4) calendar days of rest must be observed.

• If a player pitches 51 - 65 pitches in a day, three (3) calendar days of rest must be observed.

• If a player pitches 36 - 50 pitches in a day, two (2) calendar days of rest must beobserved.

• If a player pitches 21 - 35 pitches in a day, one (1) calendar days of rest must be observed.

• If a player pitches 1-20 pitches in a day, no (0) calendar day of rest is required.

f. A player may not pitch in more than one game in a day.

g. In a game suspended by darkness, weather, or other causes and resumed the following calendar day, the pitcher of record at the time the game was halted may continue to the extent of his/her eligibility, provided he/she delivered 40 or less pitches, and subject to each of these conditions:

1 . If the pitcher delivered 20 or less pitches before the game was suspended,that pitcher's pitch count will begin at zero for the continuation portion of the game;

2 . If the pitcher delivered between 21 and 40 pitches before the game was suspended, that pitcher's pitch count will begin with the number of pitches delivered in that game;

h. In a game ("Game A") suspended by darkness, weather, or other causes and resumed more than one calendar day later, the provisions of (g). above shall apply, unless the pitcher of record pitched in another game or games after Game A was halted. In that event, eligibility to pitch in the continuation portion of Game A shall be determined by the number of pitches delivered in the game or games after Game A was halted.

i. Failure to remove a pitcher who has reached his/her maximum number of pitches required by league age or use of an ineligible pitcher is basis for protest. Violation protested before the umpires leave the playing field, shall result (by actionof the Tournament Committee) in the suspension of the team's manager for the next two scheduled tournament games, even if those games are played at the next tournament level. Additional penalties (up to and including forfeiture of a game and/or disqualification of the team, managers or coaches from further tournament participation may be imposed if, in the opinion of the Tournament Committee:

1 . a manager or coach takes any action that results in making a travesty of the game,

2 . a team fails to meet the requirements of this rule more than once during the International Tournament, which begins with District play and ends at the World Series level (State level for 9-10 and 10-11), or;

3 . a manager willfully and knowingly disregards the requirements of this rule.

A manager or coach suspended for any reason is not permitted to be at the game site and must not take any part in the game, nor have any communications whatsoever with any persons at the game site. Violation may result, by action of the Tournament Committee, in further suspension, forfeiture of a game and/or disqualification of the team, managers or coaches from further tournament participation.

## 4. PITCHING RULES – SENIOR LEAGUE AND BIG LEAGUE BASEBALL

These rules replace the regular season pitching regulations. Violation of these pitching rules is subject to protest and action by the Tournament Committee in Williamsport if protested before the umpire(s) leave the playing field.

a. Any player on a tournament team may pitch. (**NOTE : There is no limit to the number of pitchers a tournament team may use in a game**.)

b. A tournament pitcher may not pitch in regular season or Special Games while the team is still participating in the tournament.

c. A pitcher remaining in the game, but moving to a different position, can return as a pitcher anytime in the remainder of the game, but only once per game.

d. The manager must remove the pitcher when said pitcher reaches the limit for his/her age group as noted below, but the pitcher may remain in the game at another position:

League Age:  1 6 – 18 (Big League) 105 pitches per day

  1 4 – 16 (Senior League) 95 pitches per day

**EXCEPTION**: If a pitcher reaches the limit imposed above for his/her league age while facing a batter, the pitcher may continue to pitch until any one of the following conditions occurs: 1. That batter reaches base; 2. That batter is put out; 3. The third out is made to complete the half-inning. **Note: A pitcher who delivers 41 or more pitches in a game cannot play the position of catcher for the remainder of that day.**

e. Pitchers league age 15-18 must adhere to the following rest requirements:

• If a player pitches 76 or more pitches in a day, four (4) calendar days of rest must be observed.

• If a player pitches 61 - 75 pitches in a day, three (3) calendar days of rest must be
observed.

• If a player pitches 46 - 60 pitches in a day, two (2) calendar days of rest must be observed.

• If a player pitches 31 -45 pitches in a day, one (1) calendar days of rest must be observed.

• If a player pitches 1-30 pitches in a day, no (0) calendar day of rest is required.

f. A player may not pitch in more than two games in a day.

g. In a game suspended by darkness, weather, or other causes and resumed the following calendar day, the pitcher of record at the time the game was halted may continue to the extent of his/her eligibility, provided he/she delivered 60 or less pitches, and subject to each of these conditions:

1 . If the pitcher delivered 30 or less pitches before the game was suspended, that pitcher's pitch count will begin at zero for the continuation portion of the game;

2 . If the pitcher delivered between 31 and 60 pitches before the game was suspended, that pitcher's pitch count will begin with the number of pitches delivered in that game;

h. In a game ("Game A") suspended by darkness, weather, or other causes and resumed more than one calendar day later, the provisions of (g.) above shall apply, unless the pitcher of record pitched in another game or games after Game A was halted. In that event, eligibility to pitch in the continuation portion of Game A shall be determined by the number of pitches delivered in the game or games after Game A was halted.

i. Failure to remove a pitcher who has reached his/her maximum number of pitches required by league age or use of an ineligible pitcher is basis for protest. Violation protested before the umpires leave the playing field, shall result (by action of the Tournament Committee) in the suspension of the team's manager for the next two scheduled tournament games, even if those games are played at the next tournament level. Additional penalties (up to and including forfeiture of a game and/or disqualification of the team, managers or coaches from further tournament participation) may be imposed if, in the opinion of the Tournament

**COMMITTEE**:

1 . a manager or coach takes any action that results in making a travesty of the game,

2 . a team fails to meet the requirements of this rule more than once during the International Tournament, which begins with District play and ends at the World Series level or;

3 . a manager willfully and knowingly disregards the requirements of this rule.

A manager or coach suspended for any reason is not permitted to be at the game site and must not take any part in the game, nor have any communications whatsoever with any persons at the game site. Violation may result, by action of the Tournament Committee, in further suspension, forfeiture of a game and/or disqualification of the team, managers or coaches from further tournament participation.

5. **FORFEITS**: No game may be forfeited or a team disqualified without the authorization of the Tournament Committee. Violations which may result in forfeiture or disqualification must be reported immediately to the Regional Director before further play takes place which would involve a

team or teams affected by such action.

6. **BENCH/DUGOUT**: No one except the players, manager and coach(es) shall occupy the bench or dugout during a game. Base coaches may be players or adults. Two (2) adult base coaches are permitted at all levels subject to playing rule 4.05 (2).

7. **VISITS**: A manager or coach may not leave a dugout for any reason during a game without receiving permission from an umpire. The manager or coach may be removed from the field for the remainder of the game for violation of this rule. When permission is granted the manager or coach will be permitted to go to the mound to confer with the pitcher or any defensive player(s). A manager or coach who is granted a time out to talk to any defensive player will be charged with a visit to the pitcher.

A manager or coach may come out twice in one inning to visit with the pitcher, but the third time out, the player must be removed as a pitcher. The manager or coach may come out three times in a game to visit with the pitcher, but the fourth time out, the player must be removed as a pitcher. The rule applies to each pitcher who enters a game.

**NOTE**: Only one offensive time-out will be permitted each inning.

8. **INJURY/ILLNESS**: If a player is injured or becomes ill during a game, the decision of a doctor (if present) or medical personnel will be final as to whether or not the player may continue in the game.

9. **MANDATORY PLAY: 9-10 Year Old Division, 10-11 Year Old Division, Little League, Junior League: Every player on a team roster shall participate in each game for a minimum of three (3) consecutive defensive outs and bat at least one (1) time.**

    a. Managers are responsible for fulfilling the mandatory play requirements.

    b. There is no exception to this rule unless the game is shortened for any reason. **NOTE**: A game is not considered shortened if the home team does not complete the offensive half of the sixth or seventh inning (or any extra inning) due to winning the game.

    c. **Failure to meet the mandatory play requirements in this rule is a basis for protest. If one or more players on a roster do not meet this requirement, and if protested before the umpires leave the playing field, it shall result (by action of the Tournament Committee) in the suspension of the team's manager for the next two scheduled tournament games, even if those games are played at the next tournament level. Additional penalties (up to and including forfeiture of a game and/or disqualification of the team, managers or coaches from further tournament participation) may be imposed if, in the opinion of the Tournament Committee:**

        1. **a manager or coach takes any action that results in making a travesty of the game, causing players to intentionally perform poorly for the purpose of extending or shortening a game, or;**

        2. **a team fails to meet the requirements of this rule more than once during the International Tournament, which begins with District play and ends at the World Series level (State level for 9-10 and 10-11), or;**

3. a manager willfully and knowingly disregards the requirements of this rule.

**A manager or coach suspended for any reason is not permitted to be at the game site and must not take any part in the game, nor have any communications whatsoever with any persons at the game site. Violation may result, by action of the Tournament Committee, in further suspension, forfeiture of a game and/or disqualification of the team, managers or coaches from further tournament participation.**

d. For the purposes of this rule, "three (3) consecutive defensive outs" is defined as: A player enters the field in one of the nine defensive positions when his/her team is on defense and occupies such position while three consecutive outs are made; "bat at least one (1) time" is defined as: A player enters the batters box with no count and completes that time at bat by being put out or by reaching base safely.

10. **SUBSTITUTIONS/RE-ENTRY**: This tournament rule replaces regular season Rule 3.03 (re-entry) for all levels of tournament play.

a. If illness, injury or the ejection of a player prevents a team from fielding nine (9) players, a player previously used in the lineup may be inserted, but only if there are no other eligible substitutes available. The opposing team manager shall select the player to re-enter the lineup. A player ejected from the game is not eligible for re-entry.

b. Any player who has been removed for a substitute may re-enter the game in the **SAME** position in the batting order.

c. **A substitute entering the game for the first time may not be removed prior to completion of her/his mandatory play requirements.**

   **NOTE 1**: See definitions in Rule 9 d above on complying with this rule defensively and offensively. Tournament Rule 10 c does not apply to Senior League or Big League Baseball.

   **NOTE 2**: A player who has met the mandatory play requirements, and is a pitcher at the time she/he is removed, may be removed for a subsitute batter and re-enter the game as a pitcher once, provided the pitcher was not physically replaced on the mound.

   **EXCEPTION: Does not apply to Senior and Big League Baseball.**

   **EXAMPLE**: Player A is a starter and not a pitcher, Player B substitutes into the game for player A. Both players have met mandatory play by completing one time at bat and 3 consecutive outs and both occupy the same spot in the batting order. In the fifth inning player A becomes a pitcher and is scheduled to bat in the sixth inning, but player B bats for player A. Both players have met mandatory play requirements and player A was not physically replaced on the mound as a pitcher, therefore, player A can return to pitch the sixth inning.

d. Defensive substitutions must be made while the team is on defense. Offensive substitutions must be made at the time the offensive player has her/his turn at bat or is on base.

e. A starter and her/his substitute must not be in the lineup at the same time, except as provided in Rule 10-a.

f.   Improper substitution is a basis for protest. Protests involving improper substitution not resolved before the next pitch or play shall not be considered.

g.   Rule 7.14, Special Pinch Runner, will apply during tournament.

h.   **Junior/Senior/Big League** only: A pitcher remaining in the game, but moving to a different position, can return as a pitcher anytime in the remainder of the game, but only once per game. **Big League only**: Rule 3.03, Designated Hitter, **WILL** apply during the tournament.

i.   **SENIOR LEAGUE/BIG LEAGUE BASEBALL**: Any player in the starting line-up, including the designated hitter, who has been removed for a substitute may re-enter the game ONCE, provided such player occupies the same batting position as he or she did in the starting line-up. A substitute (non-starter) may not reenter the game in any position once that player is removed from the line-up.

11.  **SUSPENDED GAMES**: Any game in which a winner cannot be determined in accordance with the playing rules shall be resumed from the exact point at which it was suspended regardless of the number of innings played. **EXCEPTION**: In the event that the first inning is not completed, the game shall be replayed from the beginning and all records, including pitching, disregarded. Incomplete (not regulation) or tie games are considered suspended games. **NOTE**: A contest decided by forfeit does not constitute a "game" for the purposes of this rule, unless one complete inning was physically played before the game was forfeited. (Forfeits are only by decree of the Tournament Committee in Williamsport.)

12.  **TEN-RUN RULE**: If at the end of a regulation game one team has a lead of ten (10) runs or more the manager of the team with the least runs shall concede the victory to the opponent. **NOTE**: If the visiting team has a lead of ten (10) or more runs, the home team must bat in their half of the inning.

13.  **REGULATION GAME**: Each tournament game must be played to the point of being an official game:

a.   Regulation games are of four or more innings (five or more innings for **Junior/Senior/Big League baseball**) in which one team has scored more runs than the other (three and one-half (3 1/2) (four and one-half (4 1/2) for **Junior/Senior/Big League baseball**) if the home team is ahead).

b.   Regulation games (when a winner can be determined) terminated because of weather, darkness or curfew, must **NOT** be resumed. This does not mean games suspended or delayed by weather that may still be resumed before darkness or curfew on the same day.

c.   If two games are scheduled for the same site, no "time limit" may be imposed on the first game.

14.  **REPLAYING GAMES**: No tournament game may be replayed without specific approval from the Tournament Committee at Williamsport.

15.  **UNAUTHORIZED AGREEMENTS**: No agreements shall be made between managers and/or Tournament Directors and/or umpires contrary to Tournament Rules.

16.  **ALTERCATIONS**: Any player, manager, coach or official who is involved in

a physical or verbal altercation at the game site could be suspended or removed from tournament play by the Tournament Committee.

17. **EJECTIONS**: Any manager, coach or player ejected from a game will be suspended for the next physically played game (See Rule 4.07). Ejections shall be noted in the tournament team's affidavit in the Record of Ejections on page 4. Entry should include member's name and date ejected and be signed by the Tournament Director or District Administrator.

## OFFICIALS

### Scorers

The Tournament Director having jurisdiction shall appoint and provide an official scorer for each game.

The official scorer shall, immediately following each game, enter on the reverse side of each team's Eligibility Affidavit:

1. Date of game.
2. Name of each player who pitched.
3. Number of pitches.
4. Name of opponent
5. Score of game.
6. Signature of Tournament Director or assistant. This record shall be accepted as official.

## FINANCIAL RESPONSIBILITY

Unless officially notified to the contrary by Williamsport, each league shall assume full responsibility for expenses incurred in tournament competition. Participating teams which choose not to accept housing and/or meals provided by the host shall reside and eat elsewhere at their own expense, and shall be responsible for their own local transportation.

Compensation to defray travel expenses for teams traveling beyond district competition will be paid by Little League Baseball, Incorporated, to Local Leagues in the form of a credit toward the next year's fees (U.S. leagues only). **NOTE**: A maximum of one round trip will be compensated per tournament site at each level of play. Mileage forms must be completed and submitted to Little League International by September 15, 2008, in order for reimbursement to be paid. **EXCEPTION**: The Local League president may request, in writing, reimbursement by check. This request must accompany the mileage reimbursement form.

Mileage compensation is $1 per mile. Little League International, Williamsport, Pennsylvania, will make all arrangements and reservations for transporting the regional champions to and from the World Series.

## GUIDELINES FOR CONDUCT OF TOURNAMENT

The following standards for the conduct of tournament play are for the guidance and information of Tournament Directors and participating leagues. Experience of hundreds of field directors responsible for the conduct of the tournament at all levels over many years is reflected in these guidelines which should be studied carefully and applied totally to assure successful staging of the various levels of play.

### District Administrators

District Administrators or their appointed assistants will direct the tournaments. This responsibility may not be delegated to a Local League. The Tournament Director conducts or supervises play up to and including the final game of that level; collects or directs the collection of all funds belonging to the tournament; pays or directs payments from moneys so collected or received; and makes required reports to leagues involved and to the Regional Center.

The league or leagues hosting tournaments may not assume responsibility for, nor physically operate, the tournament. The league or leagues may not retain tournament income, may not make payments from nor obligate tournament funds for any purpose.

At the district tournament meeting the Tournament Rules should be reviewed in briefing league representatives, umpires and others involved in the tournament. Before assigning tournament games, the District Administrators should inspect all prospective sites. It cannot be emphasized too strongly that providing the best possible playing conditions on regular fields is the obligation of the District Administrator.

### Tournament Director

A.  District, Sectional, Divisional, State or Regional Tournament Director may provide  appropriate awards to participating teams and players.

B.  Each Tournament Director shall report as follows:
   1.  Advise each participating league of schedule and time and site of games.
   2.  Mail completed schedule to the Regional Director showing winners at each level of play.
   3.  Pay allowable expenses and distribute balance of tournament income to the District Fund and/or leagues on a per-game basis. Where one or more teams travel greater distances than others, a mileage allowance may be paid before distributing the per-game shares.
   4.  Mail completed financial report to the Regional Director within ten (10) days following final game of each level of tournament.
       **NOTE**: 9-10 Year Old Division and 10-11 Year Old Division advances to state level only.

## Physical Conditions

It is essential that the best possible playing conditions be provided at every level of the tournament. The following conditions are recommended for tournament games:

1.  Facilities:
   a.  Grass outfield (Regional, Divisional, State and Sectional Tournaments). Grass infield (Regional, State and Divisional Tournaments).
   b.  **Outfield fences for the Little League Division must be a maximum of 225 feet from home plate and a minimum of 195 feet (Little League); For 9-10 and 10-11 divisions, a maximum of 225 feet and a minimum of 180 feet; For Junior League, a maximum of 350 feet and a minimum of 250 feet; For Senior League and Big League, a maximum of 420 feet and a minimum of 280 feet.**
   c.  Outfield fences of safe-type construction, a minimum of 4 feet in height, maximum of 6 feet.
   d.  Batter's eye 24 feet wide minimum at center field.
   e.  Backstop not less than 20 feet from home plate. Junior/Senior/Big League backstop should not be les than 35 feet from home plate.
   f.  Back drop of 6 to 8 feet of canvas in back of home plate if no press box is in that position.
   g.  Two foul poles at least 6 feet above the top of the fence.
   h.  A protective screen in front of dugouts.
   i.  Lights, if used, must meet minimum Little League standards.
   j.  Only conventional dirt pitching mounds are approved for tournament play.
2.  Groundskeeper's services:
   a.  Grass cut to proper height. No holes or other unsafe conditions.
   b.  Infield dragged and in playable condition.
   c.  Markings according to regulations.
   d.  Bases must be regulation size and properly secured.
3.  Additional Facilities:
   a.  Public address system and announcer.
   b.  Scoreboard and operator(s).

c.   Adequate seating (Sectional - 500; Divisional/State - 1,000; Regional - 1,500 minimum).

d.   Adequate parking.

e.   Policing. Local police departments should be advised of the event and requested to cooperate with league personnel.

f.   First aid, medical and ambulance services available.

g.   Rest rooms.

h.   Baseballs (if not otherwise provided by Tournament Director).

i.   Adult volunteer insurance should be provided by each league involved.

**NOTE 1**: 9-10 Year Old Divisions and 11 Year Old Divisions advances to state level only.

**NOTE 2**: Host leagues may retain concession income.

## Assistants and Committees

To assure a successful tournament, it is desirable that the director (particularly at sectional, divisional, state and regional levels) appoint assistants and committee chairpersons to undertake the various functions which are essential. The following are suggested:

1.   **Finance**: To solicit donations, supervise collections at games, sale of advertising and programs, etc. Host leagues may not conduct fund raising projects unless approved by the Tournament Director.

2.   **Housing**: Players may be housed in homes where it is possible and offers no conflict. The committee should screen and select homes, brief "foster parents" on feeding, recreation, curfew, religious requirements and time of arrival for practice and games as desired by the managers. Players, managers, coaches and umpires may be provided hotel or motel accommodations and food allowance.

3.   **Publicity**: Obtain and make available to all news media names of teams, players, time of games and sites, results of games, and other information essential to news media in the interest of promoting the tournament. Addresses and/or telephone numbers of players must not be released to anyone for any purpose.

4.   **Transportation**: Arrangements for meeting teams upon arrival and delivery to points of departure. Arrange for transportation of managers and coaches.

5.   **Program**: When authorized by the Tournament Director as a fund raising project, the Program Chairperson should work with the Finance Chairperson to assemble material, sell ads, etc. Program should not be published unless self-supporting.

6.   **Parking and Police**: If deemed necessary, arrange for traffic control, parking and related functions.

7.   **Medical**: Have names and phone numbers of doctors, nurses, ambulance and hospital available and arrangements made for their services, if required. If possible, a doctor or nurse should be in attendance.

8.   **Ceremonies**: Arrange for flag raising, welcome, introductions, etc. These should be brief and meaningful.

9.   **Umpires**: Recommended minimum of two, a maximum of six. Services

on a voluntary basis. Normal expenses may be provided.

10. **Official scorekeepers**.

## Expenses

Tournament Directors are authorized to pay from tournament income the following costs:

1. Championship pennant.
2. Approved Little League pins for players, managers, coaches (all teams) and umpires.
3. Postage, telephone and out-of-pocket expenses.
4. Housing and food allowance for players, managers, coaches and umpires.
   NOTE: Tournament Director should secure, at no cost to the tournament, baseballs (if not provided by host league), umpires, scorekeepers and housing for players.

## Radio

Broadcasting of tournament games is permitted with authorization from the Tournament Director. Commercial sponsorship must be consistent with Little League policy. Fees or donations paid for the broadcasting rights must accrue to the tournament fund at that level.

## Television

Only Little League Headquarters may authorize the televising (live or taped) of tournament games. The District Administrator or Tournament Director may recommend approval, but may not make commitments or sign any agreement or contracts for the televising of games.

Not later than two weeks prior to the start of the tournament at the level to be televised, the director having jurisdiction shall submit in writing complete details of the proposal to Little League Headquarters. Video taping of games is permissible provided tapes are not sold or used for any commercial purposes.

Brief, televised reports on tournament games and activities on news programs are permitted.

## Programs

The District Administrator or Tournament Director may authorize the publication of a program or scorecard as a means of providing additional financing for the tournament at that level. However, they may not execute contracts or other commitments in the name of, or as agents for, Little League International. All funds (net) realized from advertising and/or sale of programs must be applied to the tournament fund at that level.

## REGIONAL DIRECTORS

The following Regional Directors or their appointed agents should be contacted by the Tournament Director when protests cannot be resolved at the tournament level.

### U.S. EAST
Director - Don Soucy; Assistant Director - Corey Wright;
Assistant Director - Pat Holden
P.O. Box 2926; Bristol, CT 06011; PHONE: 860-585-4730

### U.S. CENTRAL
Director - Mike Legge; Assistant Director - Nina Johnson
9802 E. Little League Drive; Indianapolis, IN 46235
PHONE: 317-897-6127

### U.S. SOUTHEAST
Director - Jennifer Colvin; Assistant Director- Peter Frikker
PO Box 7557; Warner Robins, GA; PHONE: 478-971-7070

### U.S. WEST
Director - James Gerstenslager; Assistant Director - Dave Bonham;
Assistant Director - Brent Stahlnecker
6707 Little League Drive; San Bernardino, CA 92407; PHONE: 909-887-6444

### U.S. SOUTHWEST
Director - Mike Witherwax
P.O. Box 20127; Waco, TX 76702; PHONE: 254-756-1816

# INTERNATIONAL TOURNAMENT POOL PLAY FORMAT
## SECTION I – GUIDELINES

The Pool Play Format should only be used in divisions in which there is a reasonable expectation for all teams to play all games for which they are scheduled. In divisions in which teams traditionally drop out at the last moment, or partway through the tournament, the standard double-elimination or single-elimination formats should be used instead.

The following conditions must apply to all Pool Play Format tournaments, unless specified as optional:

A. In the event a team or teams drop out of a pool play format tournament before the first game of the tournament is played (by any team in the tournament), the pools must be redrawn. If a team or teams drop out or is/are removed by action of the Tournament Committee after the first game is played, the matter must be referred to the Tournament Committee for a decision.

B. A Pool Play Format tournament may have one or more pools.

C. The pool assignments (or "draw") must either be a blind draw, or must be based on geographic considerations. Pool assignments must never be "seeded" based on the expected ability of the teams.

D. In all cases, the results of Pool Play have no bearing on the next segment of play, with the exception of rules and regulations regarding rest periods for pitchers, (i.e., losses do not "carry over").

E. It is preferable for each team in a given pool to be scheduled to play all other teams in that pool once.

F. Each team within any one pool must be scheduled to play an equal number of games as the other teams in that pool.

G. In the case of a one-pool tournament, one team may advance to become the tournament champion, based solely on the results of pool play, at the discretion of the tournament director. More commonly in a one-pool tournament, however, two teams advance to play each other for the tournament championship.

H. If more than one pool is used, and the total number of teams in the largest and smallest of the pools combined is less than ten (10), the number of teams in largest pool must be no more than one team greater than the number of teams in the smallest pool. Example:

| Acceptable | | Not Acceptable | |
|---|---|---|---|
| Pool A | Pool B | Pool A | Pool B |
| 4 teams | 5 teams | 3 teams | 6 teams |

I. If more than one pool is used, and the total number of teams in the largest and smallest of the pools is ten (10) or more, the number of teams in the largest pool must be no more than two teams greater than the number of teams in smallest pool. Example:

| Acceptable | | Not Acceptable | |
|---|---|---|---|
| Pool A | Pool B | Pool A | Pool B |
| 4 teams | 6 teams | 3 teams | 7 teams |

J. In the case of tournaments involving more than one pool, one or more teams may advance out of each pool to the next segment. In most cases, when two teams advance, the schedule may be arranged so that teams will "cross over" for the purpose of seeding in the next round. For example, in a two-pool tournament:

    1. The first-place team in Pool A plays the second-place team in Pool B.

    2. The first-place team in Pool B plays the second-place team in Pool A.

    3. The winners of those two games play each other for the championship.

    4. A consolation game may be scheduled between the losing teams. The crossover method, however, is not required. At the discretion of the tournament director, the teams advancing from pool play could be re-drawn for placement in the next round via blind draw.

K.    In the case of tournaments involving more than one team advancing out of pool play into a playoff, the playoff format may be single- or double-elimination, at the discretion of the tournament director.

However, if the published format calls for double-elimination, and the tournament director subsequently wishes for it to revert to single-elimination because of delays caused by weather, etc., this can only be approved by the Tournament Committee in Williamsport.

L.    The tournament director may, at his/her discretion, use a format in which all teams that finish the pool play round with a specific won-lost record will advance. In the following examples, the format calls for advancing all teams (from a 10-team pool in which each team plays only seven games) that finish pool play with zero or one loss. Example 1: Among the 10 teams in the pool, two finished with 7-0 records, while two others finished with 6-1 records. Result – These four teams advance and the other six teams are eliminated. Example 2: Among the 10 teams in the pool, one finished with a 7-0 record, while two others finished with 6-1 records. Result – These three teams advance and the other seven teams are eliminated.

M.    The tiebreaker methods published herein by Little League International are the only methods that will be used when a tiebreaker is required. If any question or controversy arises, it must be referred to the Regional Headquarters before advancing a team.

N.    A manager is not permitted to purposely forfeit any game for the purpose of engineering the outcome of pool play, and may be removed from the tournament by action of the Tournament Committee in Williamsport. Additionally, the Tournament Committee may remove such a team from further tournament play.

O.    Only the Tournament Committee can forfeit a game in the International Tournament, and reserves the right to disregard the results of a forfeited game in computing a team's won-lost record and Runs-Allowed Ratio. (Section IV)

P.    When a manager or coach instructs his/her players to play poorly for any reason, such as, but not limited to the following, such action may result in the manager's removal by the umpire-in-chief, and/or removal of the manager, coach(es) and/or team from further tournament play. Note – This policy is not intended to prevent a manager from using lesser-skilled players more frequently if he or she wishes, even if such action may result in losing a game):

> 1. losing a game to effect a particular outcome in a Pool Play Format tournament;
>
> 2. so as to lose a game by the 10-run rule;
>
> 3. to delay the game until the curfew;
>
> 4. to allow an opponent to tie the score so that more innings may be played, etc.

### SECTION II – SEGMENTS OF A POOL PLAY TOURNAMENT

A. Under this format, there are two distinct segments to a pool play format tournament.

> 1. In Segment 1 – The Pool Play Round, the teams are divided into a number of pools (usually two to four pools). Each team in each of the pools should play the other teams in that pool once. By decision of the tournament director, one or more teams with the best records(s) in the pool will advance to the next segment. Note: In a one-pool format, one or more teams team may advance to become the tournament champion. If only one team advances, there is no second segment.
>
> 2. In Segment 2 – The Elimination Round, the teams advancing out of Segment 1 are matched up in either a standard single-elimination format, or a standard double-elimination format.

B. Once a segment is completed, games played previously have no bearing on the next segment, with the exception of:

> 1. rules and regulations regarding the required rest periods for pitchers;
>
> 2. rules and regulations regarding players, managers and/or coaches that were ejected, and the prescribed penalties resulting from the ejection.

### SECTION III – TIEBREAKER PROCEDURES

A. In all cases, the team(s) advancing past Segment 1 must be the team(s) with the best won-lost record(s) during pool play. The tournament director will decide the number of teams that will advance beyond pool play, and such decision must be made available to the leagues/teams involved before the tournament begins.

B. When records are tied, however, the following procedures must be applied in order, so that the tie can be broken. These procedures also apply to determining the seeding for Segment 2 (the playoff round), if seeding for Segment 2 is based on results of pool play.

> 1. The first tiebreaker is the result of the head-to-head match-up(s) during pool play (Segment 1) of the teams that are involved in the tie.
>
> > a) If one of the teams involved in the tie has accomplished EVERY ONE of the following, then that team will advance:
> >
> > i. Defeated all of the other teams involved in the tie at

least once, AND;

ii. Defeated all of the other teams involved in the tie in every one of the pool play games it played against those teams; AND;

iii. Played each of the teams involved in the tie an equal number of times.

example: Three teams are tied with identical records for first place at the end of pool play, and one team is to advance to Segment 2. Teams A, B and C played against each other once in pool play. Team A won all of its games against Team B and Team C during pool play. Result – Team A advances, while Team B and Team C are eliminated.

b) Each time a tie is broken to advance one team, leaving a tie between two or more teams, the situation reverts to "B. 1." (head-to-head results) in this section.

1. Example: Three teams are tied with identical records for first place at the end of pool play, and two teams are to advance to Segment 2. Teams A, B and C played against each other once in pool play. Team A won all of its games against Team B and Team C during pool play. Result – Team A advances, which then creates a two-way tie between Team B and Team C. That tie then is broke by reverting to "B. 1. a)" in this section.

2. If the results of the head-to-head match-up(s) during pool play of the teams that are involved in the tie cannot break the tie (because no team defeated each of the other teams in the tie each time they played, or because no team has defeated all of the other teams involved in the tie in everyone of the pool play games played between those teams, or because the teams involved in the tie did not play one another an equal number of times during pool play), then the tie is broken using the Runs-Allowed Ratio (see Section IV).

C. In all cases, if the tie-breaking principles herein are correctly applied and fail to break the tie, or if these guidelines are not applied correctly (in the judgment of the Tournament Committee in Williamsport), then the matter will be referred to the Tournament Committee, which will be the final arbiter in deciding the issue. If a tie cannot be broken through the proper application of these guidelines (in the opinion of the Tournament Committee), then a playoff, blind draw or coin flip will determine which team(s) will advance. This is a decision of the Tournament Committee.

## SECTION IV – RUNS-ALLOWED RATIO

A. For each team involved in a tie in which head-to-head results cannot be used (because no team defeated each of the other teams in the tie each time they played, or because no team has defeated all of the other teams involved in the tie in everyone of the pool play games played between those teams, or because the teams involved in the tie did not play one another an equal number of times during pool play), the tournament director will calculate: The total number of runs given up in all pool play games played by that team, divided by the number of half-innings played on defense in pool play games by that team. This provides the number of runs give up per half-inning by that team: the Runs-Allowed Ratio.

1. Example: The Hometown Little League team has given up eight (8) runs in all four (4) of its pool play games, and has played 23 innings on defense in those four games. 8 divided by 23 equals .3478

2. The Runs-Allowed Ratio for Hometown Little League (.3478 in the example above) is compared to the same calculation for each of the teams involved in the tie.

B. The Runs-Allowed Ratio is used to advance ONLY ONE team.

C. If, after computing the Runs-Allowed Ratio using results of all pool play games played by the teams involved in the tie:

1. one team has the lowest Runs-Allowed Ratio, that team advances. After one team has advanced using the Runs-Allowed Ratio, the breaking of any other ties must revert to the methods detailed in Section III – Tiebreaker Procedures, before the Runs-Allowed Ratio is used to break the tie.

2. two or more teams remain tied, and the methods detailed in Section III – Tiebreaker Procedures cannot be used (because no team defeated each of the other teams in the tie each time they played, or because no team has defeated all of the other teams involved in the tie in everyone of the pool play games played between those teams, or because the teams involved in the tie did not play one another an equal number of times during pool play), then the Runs-Allowed Ratio must be recomputed using statistics only from the pool play games played between the teams involved in the tie. The results are used to advance ONE team, and any other ties must revert to the methods detailed in Section III – Tiebreaker Procedures, before the Runs-Allowed Ratio is used to break the tie.

D. Any part of a half-inning played on defense will count as a complete half-inning on defense for the purposes of computing the Runs-Allowed Ratio.

E. If a game is forfeited, in most cases the score of the game will be recorded as 6-0 (for Little League Divisions and below) or 7-0 (for Junior League Divisions and above). However, only the Tournament Committee in Williamsport can decree a forfeit, and the Tournament Committee reserves the right to disregard the results of the game, to assign the score as noted above, or to allow the score to stand (if any part of the game was played).

F. If a game is forfeited, in most cases each team involved in the forfeit will be deemed to have played six defensive half-innings (for Little League Divisions and below) or seven defensive innings (for Junior League Divisions and above). However, forfeits and the final score and number of innings charged or credited in forfeits, can only be decreed by the Tournament Committee in Williamsport.

G. In the event a team (defined for this purpose as a minimum of nine players) fails to attend a scheduled game, and it is determined by the Tournament Committee in Williamsport that the failure to attend was designed to cause a forfeit or delay the tournament for any reason, the

Tournament Committee reserves the right to remove the team from further play in the International Tournament and/or remove those adults it deems responsible from the team and/or local league.

## APPENDIX A
## LIGHTNING SAFETY GUIDELINES

Each year across the United States, thunderstorms produce an estimated 25 million cloud-to-ground flashes of lightning - each one of those flashes is a potential killer. According to the National Weather Service, an average of 73 people are killed by lightning each year and hundreds more are injured, some suffering devastating neurological injuries that persist for the rest of their lives. A growing percentage of those struck are involved in outside recreational activities.

Officials responsible for sports events often lack adequate knowledge of thunderstorms and lightning to make educated decisions on when to seek safety. Without knowledge, officials base their decisions on personal experience and, sometimes, on the desire to complete the activity. Due to the nature of lightning, personal experience can be misleading.

While many people routinely put their lives in jeopardy when thunderstorms are nearby, few are actually struck by lightning. This results in a false sense of safety. Unfortunately, this false sense of safety has resulted in numerous lightning deaths and injuries during the past several decades because people made decisions that unknowingly put their lives or the lives of others at risk.

For organized outdoor activities, the National Weather Service recommends those in charge have a lightning safety plan, and that they follow the plan without exception. The plan should give clear and specific safety guidelines in order to eliminate errors in judgment. Prior to an activity or event, organizers should listen to the latest forecast to determine the likelihood of thunderstorms. NOAA Weather Radio is a good source of up-to-date weather information. Once people start to arrive, the guidelines in your league's lightning safety plan should be followed.

A thunderstorm is approaching or nearby. Are conditions safe, or is it time to head for safety? Not wanting to appear overly cautious, many people wait far too long before reacting to this potentially deadly weather threat. The safety recommendations outlined here based on lightning research and the lessons learned from the unfortunate experiences of thousands of lightning strike victims.

Thunderstorms produce two types of lightning flashes, 'negative' and 'positive.' While both types are deadly, the characteristics of the two are quite different. Negative flashes occur more frequently, usually under or near the base of the thunderstorm where rain is falling. In contrast, positive flashes generally occur away from the center of the storm, often in areas where rain is not falling. There is no place outside that is safe in or near a thunderstorm. Consequently, people need to stop what they are doing and get to a safe place immediately. Small outdoor buildings including dugouts, rain shelters, sheds, etc., are NOT SAFE. Substantial buildings with wiring and plumbing provide the greatest amount of protection. Office buildings,

schools, and homes are examples of buildings that
would offer protection. Once inside, stay away from windows and doors
and anything that conducts electricity such as corded phones, wiring,
plumbing, and
anything connected to these. In the absence of a substantial building,
a hard-topped metal vehicle with the windows closed provides good
protection. Occupants should avoid contact with metal in the vehicle and,
to the extent possible, move away from windows.

### Who should monitor the weather and who is responsible for making the decision to stop activities?

Lightning safety plans should specify that someone be designated to
monitor the weather for lightning. The 'lightning monitor' should not
include the coaches, umpires, or referees, as they are not able to devote
the attention needed to adequately monitor conditions. The 'lightning
monitor' must know the plan's guidelines and be empowered to assure that
those guidelines are followed.

### When should activities be stopped?

The sooner activities are stopped and people get to a safe place, the greater
the level of safety. In general, a significant lightning threat extends outward
from the base of a thunderstorm cloud about 6 to 10 miles. Therefore,
people should move to a safe place when a thunderstorm is 6 to 10 miles
away. Also, the plan's guidelines should account for the time it will take for
everyone to get to a safe place. Here are some criteria that could be used to
halt activities.
1. If lightning is observed. The ability to see lightning varies depending
on the time of day, weather conditions, and obstructions such as trees,
mountains,
etc. In clear air, and especially at night, lightning can be seen from storms
more than 10 miles away provided that obstructions don't limit the view of
the thunderstorm.
2. If thunder is heard. Thunder can usually be heard from a distance of
about 10 miles provided that there is no background noise. Traffic, wind,
and precipitation may limit the ability to hear thunder less than 10 miles
away. If you hear thunder, though, it's a safe bet that the storm is within ten
miles.
3. If the time between lightning and corresponding thunder is 30 seconds
or less. This would indicate that the thunderstorm is 6 miles away or less.
As with the previous two criteria, obstructions, weather, noise and other
factors may limit the ability to use this criterion. In addition, a designated
person must diligently monitor any lightning. In addition to any of the
above criteria, activities should be halted if the sky looks threatening.
Thunderstorms can develop directly overhead and some storms may
develop lightning just as they move into an area.

### When should activities be resumed?

Because electrical charges can linger in clouds after a thunderstorm has
passed, experts agree that people should wait at least 30 minutes after the

storm before resuming activities.

**What should be done if someone is struck by lightning?**
Most lightning strike victims can survive a lightning strike; however, medical attention may be needed immediately - have someone call for medical help. Victims do not carry an electrical charge and should be attended to at once. In many cases, the victim's heart and/or breathing may have stopped and CPR may be needed to revive them. The victim should continue to be monitored until medical help arrives; heart and/or respiratory problems could persist, or the victim could go into shock. If possible, move the victim to a safer place away from the threat of another lightning strike.

## APPENDIX B
## SAFETY CODE FOR LITTLE LEAGUE

- Responsibility for safety procedures should be that of an adult member of the local league.
- Arrangements should be made in advance of all games and practices for emergency medical services.
- Managers, coaches and umpires should have some training in first-aid. First-Aid Kit should be available at the field.
- No games or practice should be held when weather or field conditions are not good, particularly when lighting is inadequate. (See Lightning Safety Guidelines.)
- Play area should be inspected frequently for holes, damage, glass and other foreign objects.
- Dugouts and bat racks should be positioned behind screens.
- Only players, managers, coaches and umpires are permitted on the playing field during play and practice sessions.
- Responsibility for keeping bats and loose equipment off the field of play should be that of a regular player assigned for this purpose.
- Procedure should be established for retrieving foul balls batted out of the playing area.
- During practice sessions and games, all players should be alert and watching the batter on each pitch.
- During warm up drills, players should be spaced so that no one is endangered by errant balls.
- Equipment should be inspected regularly. Make sure it fits properly.
- Pitching machines, if used, must be in good working order (including extension cords, outlets, etc.) and must be operated only by adult managers and coaches.
- Batters must wear protective NOCSAE helmets during practice, as well as during games.
- Catchers must wear catcher's helmet (with face mask and throat guard), chest protector and shin guards. Male catchers must wear long-model chest protector (divisions below Junior League), protective supporter and cup at all times.
- Except when runner is returning to a base, head first slides are not permitted. This applies only to Little League (Majors), Minor League

and Tee Ball.
- At no time should "horse play" be permitted on the playing field.
- Parents of players who wear glasses should be encouraged to provide "Safety Glasses."
- Players must not wear watches, rings, pins, jewelry or other metallic items.
- Catchers must wear catcher's helmet, face mask and throat guard in warming up pitchers. This applies between innings and in bull pen practice. Skull caps are not permitted.
- Batting/catcher's helmets should not be painted unless approved by the manufacturer.
- Regulations prohibit on-deck batters. This means no player should handle a bat, even while in an enclosure, until it is his/her time at bat. This applies only to Little League (Majors), Minor League and Tee Ball. This applies only to Little League (Majors), Minor League and Tee Ball.
- Players who are ejected, ill or injured should remain under supervision until released to the parent or guardian.

## APPENDIX C
## COMMUNICABLE DISEASE PROCEDURES

While risk of one athlete infecting another with HIV/AIDS during competition is close to non-existent, there is a remote risk that other blood born infectious diseases can be transmitted. For example, Hepatitis B can be present in blood as well as in other body fluids. Procedures for reducing the potential for transmission of these infectious agents should include, but not be limited to, the following:

1. The bleeding must be stopped, the open wound covered and if there is an excessive amount of blood on the uniform it must be changed before the athlete may participate.

2. Routine use of gloves or other precautions to prevent skin and mucous-membrane exposure when contact with blood or other body fluids is anticipated.

3. Immediately wash hands and other skin surfaces if contaminated (in contact) with blood or other body fluids. Wash hands immediately after removing gloves.

4. Clean all contaminated surfaces and equipment with an appropriate disinfectant before competition resumes.

5. Practice proper disposal procedures to prevent injuries caused by needles, scalpels and other sharp instruments or devices.

6. Although saliva has not been implicated in HIV transmission, to minimize the need for emergency mouth-to-mouth resuscitation, mouthpieces, resuscitation bags, or other ventilation devices should be available for use.

7. Athletic trainers/coaches with bleeding or oozing skin conditions should refrain from all direct athletic care until the condition resolves.

8. Contaminated towels should be properly disposed of/disinfected.

9. Follow acceptable guidelines in the immediate control of bleeding and when handling bloody dressings, mouthguards and other articles containing body fluids.

Additional information is available from your state high school association and from the National Federation TARGET program.

## APPENDIX D
## BAT MODIFICATIONS AND ALTERATIONS

While Little League International has not received any reports of Little League volunteers or players making alterations to bats designed to increase their performance, it has been an issue in some upper levels of play.

In an effort to ensure this does not become a problem in Little League, this policy statement has been prepared.

No bat, in any level of Little League Baseball or Softball play, is permitted to be altered, This is of particular concern especially when it is clearly done to enhance performance and violate bat standards. Making such alterations to bats is clearly an inappropriate attempt to gain an unfair advantage, and cheating has no place in our program. Umpires, managers and coaches are instructed to inspect bats before games and practices - as they always should - to determine if bats might have been altered.

This includes using the appropriate Little League Bat Ring. If a bat does not clearly pass through the correct size ring, or if it has a flat spot on it, the bat must not be used. (This may simply indicate the bat has become misshapen with use, and does not necessarily indicate it was purposely altered. Still, the bat must be removed.)

Other signs to look for include contorted or mangled end-caps or knobs on non-wood bats. This could indicate that machinery was used to "shave" the inside of the bat to make it lighter. Bats with evidence of this type of tampering also must not be used.

Little League International wishes to make it clear that tampering with bats (or any other piece of equipment) is dangerous, and the equipment must not be used in any Little League game or practice.